Competence, Admissions, and Articulation:
Returning to the Basics in Higher Education

by Jean L. Preer

ASHE-ERIC Higher Education Research Report No. 6, 1983

Prepared by

 ® *Clearinghouse on Higher Education*
The George Washington University

Published by

ASHE

Association for the Study of Higher Education

Jonathan D. Fife,
Series Editor

Cite as:
Preer, Jean L. *Competence, Admissions, and Articulation: Returning to the Basics in Higher Education.* ASHE-ERIC Higher Education Research Report No. 6. Washington, D.C.: Association for the Study of Higher Education, 1983.

The ERIC Clearinghouse on Higher Education invites individuals to submit proposals for writing monographs for the Higher Education Research Report series. The proposal must address an issue of national importance and be designed to develop a bridge between research and institutional practices. Manuscripts should be 120 to 140 pages in length. Proposals must include:
1. A detailed manuscript proposal of not more than five pages.
2. A 75-word summary to be used by several review committees for the initial screening and rating of each proposal.
3. A vita.
4. A writing sample.

ISSN 0737-1292
ISBN 0-913317-05-5

ERIC **Clearinghouse on Higher Education**
The George Washington University
One Dupont Circle, Suite 630
Washington, D.C. 20036

Association for the Study of Higher Education
One Dupont Circle, Suite 630
Washington, D.C. 20036
(202) 296-2597

This publication was prepared with funding from the National Institute of Education, U.S. Department of Education, under contract no. 400-82-0011. The opinions expressed in this report do not necessarily reflect the positions or policies of NIE or the Department.

CONTENTS

FOREWORD

We recommend that schools, colleges, and universities adopt more rigorous and measurable standards, and higher expectations, for academic performance and student conduct, and that four-year colleges and universities raise their requirements for admission. This will help students do their best educationally with challenging materials in an environment that supports learning and authentic accomplishment. (National Commission . . . , 1983, p. 27).

This was the second recommendation of the National Commission on Excellence in Education as presented in their report, *A Nation at Risk: The Imperative for Educational Reform*. In making this recommendation, the Commission clearly articulated its belief in the interrelated responsibility between elementary/secondary schools and higher education in establishing standards and expectations for students' academic performance.

This interrelationship can be traced throughout the cyclical history of American education. Until the establishment of a broad-based publicly-supported elementary and secondary school system, colleges were, in part, dependent for their students upon private tutors or, primarily, their college-run preparatory schools. Institutions therefore had direct control over the educational development of the students being admitted. With the rise of public high schools, colleges increasingly lost that control and had to adapt to the educational background of the high school graduates. As colleges became dissatisfied with high school standards, they relied more heavily on standardized tests, (e.g. Scholastic Aptitude Tests and the American College Tests) to screen their applicants. Reliance on these tests allowed higher education institutions to regain some control over acceptable applicant qualifications. The tests also provided high schools with academic standards to use in adjusting their own curricula. The turbulent 1960s drastically influenced academic standards and expectations, and saw higher education institutions again lose their control. With affirmative action and equal educational opportunity accepted as part of the education mission, rigorous admissions standards decreased.

Three other conditions also contributed to the lowering of academic performance. First was an experimentation with learning theory coupled with student demands for more "socially relevant" courses. Second was a combination of economic and social conditions. In particular, low wages, lack of public support concerning discipline, and heavier workloads contributed to a de-professionalizing of elementary secondary teaching. As a consequence, fewer top students entered the teaching profession at a time when more qualified and dedicated teachers were leaving. Third, as the college-bound pool of students began to decrease, many institutions lowered their admissions standards to maintain student enrollments.

Society, through various study groups and national commissions, is now expressing strong dissatisfaction with the results of this trend. Increasingly there is a call for:

- Return to basic education,
- Increased use of competence-based standards to justify high school graduation, and
- Raising of college admissions standards.

These issues are skillfully addressed by Dr. Jean Preer. By examining the issues of competency testing, standardized testing, and new measures of achievement and competency in college, Dr. Preer clearly identifies the major issues, responses, and consequences. This report will be immensely useful as high schools, state boards of education, and higher education institutions review their role in raising our nation's academic standards.

Jonathan D. Fife
Director and Series Editor
ERIC Clearinghouse on Higher Education
The George Washington University

EXECUTIVE SUMMARY

The preparation of American students for college seems to
have lost ground on nearly every front. In the past, a
student's movement through high school into college
depended on successful completion of required courses
and prescribed numbers of units. While high school grades
crept upward, however, nationwide aptitude test scores
declined steadily. A diploma no longer indicated that the
graduate had acquired the skills or mastered the subjects
once associated with readiness for higher education. Even
selective institutions were forced to undertake remedial programs for students ill equipped to handle college-level work.

At the same time, a diverse group of new students
sought access to higher education without the traditional
numerical indicators of college success. Admissions
officers sought alternative criteria by which to gauge a
student's potential. Legislators and educators faced an
increasingly complex set of issues affecting new and
traditional students, low and high achievers, basic and
higher-order skills.

*Returning to
the basics may
involve new
complexity
rather than
old simplicity.*

Reports by the National Commission on Excellence in
Education, task forces of the Southern Regional Education
Board, the Twentieth Century Fund, and the Education
Commission of the States have reached a consensus
concerning the magnitude of the problem and the need for
significant action. Specialists have reported the deterioration of instruction at all levels in the humanities, foreign
languages, science, and mathematics and the inadequate
preparation and shortages of teachers in those areas.

A concern for quality and coherence is returning to
American education at the high school and college levels.
But the extent to which American education can respond
to the declining performance of students nationwide will
depend on new curricular strategies, new measures of
assessment, and new cooperation between schools,
colleges, communities, state legislatures, and the federal
government. Policy makers have already begun to tackle
these fundamental issues:

- What skills and subjects are basic?
- How do schools enhance and measure competence?
- Who is responsible for setting higher standards?

Returning to the basics may involve new complexity rather
than old simplicity. Despite setbacks over the last two

decades, American education has made notable gains, especially in increasing the access of all students to higher education and in responding to the diverse needs these students bring. Efforts to regain lost ground must also guard against retreat in these areas.

Secondary schools and colleges currently face similar, major questions. Despite the differences in student bodies and institutional missions at the two levels, efforts to return to the basics will encounter common problems and will require cooperative action.

What Skills and Subjects Are Basic?
Efforts have begun in both high schools and in colleges to identify what skills and subject mastery are essential at each level. Their methods have in common a return to more rigorous and coherent course requirements, clearer and more specific performance standards, and additional remedial work for students falling behind.

At the high school level, these measures have taken the form of minimum competence testing and stiffer course requirements for graduation. The movement to minimum competence testing in the late 1970s was the first major response to the declining performance of American high school students. Often initiated by state legislators rather than by educators, minimum competence testing meant established standards in basic skills, usually reading, writing, and mathematics, necessary to function independently as an adult. More than two-thirds of the states have adopted some variation of competence testing, either for diagnostic or placement purposes or as a condition for promotion or graduation. Most include remedial programs to help students attain the required level of skills. The trend is to establish levels of skills and to start competence testing in the elementary grades.

Minimum competence testing may adversely affect both academically able and educationally disadvantaged students. Education centered around basic skills may short-change students with high abilities. Testing as a condition of graduation may deprive disproportionate numbers of minority students of a high school diploma. In suits by black students challenging such tests, implementation has been delayed in previously segregated school systems, and officials have been required to establish that the tests actually examine what is taught in schools. Nevertheless, when these conditions have been met, courts have upheld the requirement for a test before graduation.

Competence testing is oriented toward skills at a fairly low level, often around 9th grade. Schools are also instituting new subject-oriented requirements for graduation. The trend is for local school districts to raise the number of courses required in English, science, and mathematics. The Advisory Panel on the Scholastic Aptitude Test Score Decline attributed some of the apparent drop to the proliferation of high school courses, relaxation in the number of required courses, and dilution in course content. School districts and state boards are already moving in what the National Commission on Excellence in Education termed the "five basics": four years of English, three years each of mathematics, science, and social studies, and one-half year of computer science. Similarly, Project EQuality of the College Board has formulated basic academic competencies and a basic academic curriculum detailing skills and content mastery for college-bound students. They are seen as interdependent and fundamental aspects of preparation for college. A number of state agencies and educational institutions are already using Project EQuality in setting standards and revising curricula.

How Do Schools Enhance and Measure Competence?
In an earlier era, the level of performance required by minimum competence testing might have been sufficient, but at a time when more than half of all high school graduates go on to college, it is an unsatisfactory and anachronistic goal. High schools must provide increasingly sophisticated training for college-bound students. Traditionally the success of these students has been measured internally by grade point average and class rank. It has been gauged externally by scores on national standardized tests of aptitude, such as those of the Educational Testing Service and the American College Testing Program. Taken together, they provide the best predictor of a student's likely success during the first year of college.

The limitations of all these measures have been questioned, particularly the fairness of standardized test scores for minority youth. In the past, groups such as the NAACP sought to correct cultural bias in the tests, to involve blacks in developing the tests, and to prevent the inappropriate use of test scores. Recently, the NAACP has instituted a program to improve low-income black students' performance on the SAT and the ACT. Testing legislation at the state level has had mixed results: test administrations have been cut back, and the testing industry has undertaken greater self-regulation. The Committee on Ability Testing of the National Research Council has opposed the regulation of testing at the federal level as has the testing industry itself.

Too many colleges continue to require students to take standardized admissions tests, although research shows that only a few institutions rely on the results for decisions about admissions. Two-year colleges and nonselective four-year colleges should examine their test requirements and consider alternative methods of diagnostic and placement testing after a student has enrolled. Admissions officers at more selective institutions weigh a variety of factors, the most important being high school record, test scores, and pattern of high school subjects.

Although the trend is for colleges to stiffen their admissions requirements, many admissions officers, particularly at the most selective institutions, often prefer flexible admissions policies. Balancing stiffer requirements for admission with flexible admissions policies will be a major challenge of the 1980s. The use of inflexible cutoff scores on standardized tests is widely criticized. The 1983 NCAA Rule 48, which established an SAT/ACT cutoff score, minimum grade point average, and course requirements for intercollegiate athletes, demonstrates the dangers of undue rigidity for minority and low-income students. Even selective private institutions, which profess to value nonquantifiable personal qualities in evaluating applicants, need to do a better job. Institutions should consider how their admissions policies fit the school's academic mission and should provide better information to applicants on the significance of different criteria for admission. Admissions will increasingly be part of institutional development in the 1980s with targeted recruiting and a new emphasis on attracting high-ability students.

Some colleges are considering new methods of measuring the competence of both applicants and students. They include the use of standardized achievement tests, now taken by only a small number of the most able students, as an alternative to aptitude tests. It is argued that this practice would encourage students to take their high school courses more seriously and schools to upgrade their curricula in anticipation of subject-oriented examinations. Colleges have also experimented with new course requirements, including foreign languages, for graduation. Some have adopted competence-based curricula and instituted competence tests for admission to the upper division. The trend to more coherent general education requirements or to a core curriculum is another commonly reported response at the college level. Some institutions have employed the value-added approach to measure the performance of students and the effectiveness of programs. By determining the progress of students over time, the value-added approach provides a dynamic indicator of achievement that can be used with various types of assessment instruments and at different types of institutions.

Who Is Responsible for Setting Higher Standards?
The return to quality and coherence in American education must involve educators at the college, high school, and elementary levels and policy makers in federal, state, and local governments. Changes are already underway in each sector. The federal government has sounded a call to action. State boards of higher education are raising requirements for admission to state universities; school boards are stiffening requirements for graduation from high school. Often, however, the very autonomy of these separate sectors makes the realignment of standards more difficult.

The interrelated nature of the various parts of the education system is increasingly appreciated. If we are to achieve what Jerome Bruner described as the spiral curriculum, the links between programs, skills, and expectations at every level will have to be clarified and strengthened. Educators, legislators, and the public are newly aware of the seriousness of the problems they jointly face. A return to the basics—quality and coherence—will require long-term adjustments in standards, preparation of students and teachers, methods of assessment, and institutional cooperation.

COMPETENCE TESTING

The trend toward minimum competence testing of the late 1970s now seems an established part of educational assessment in American elementary and secondary schools. The legislation and programs implementing minimum standards for competence vary across the nation, with what some call "dizzying diversity" (Neill 1978, p. 41). The 1981 survey by the Educational Commission of the States described minimum competence testing, either for assessing students' progress or as a requirement for promotion or graduation, in 38 states (Pipho 1981). Despite the variety of standards, common characteristics can be identified. They include mastery of basic, defined skills for placement or for passage through the educational system, frequent testing of those skills, and the provision of support services for students whose skills fall below the minimum standard. Experience over the last five years has demonstrated the complexities involved in "returning to the basics." Educators and policy makers have struggled to define what skills are basic, how those skills are to be measured, and how schools are to use the results of minimum competence testing.

Proponents of minimum competence testing emphasize the benefits of bringing all students up to a minimum level of performance (Lerner 1981). Opponents warn against minimum standards' becoming maximum standards (Wharton 1979). They caution against the adverse effects of minimum standards on students with special needs—the educationally or economically disadvantaged, those for whom English is a second language, the handicapped—as well as on students of outstanding academic ability. The results of the first wave of competence testing are just being felt.

The impetus for minimum competence testing sets it apart from other major educational innovations of the last two decades. First, demands for change came not from educators and professionals but from legislators and citizens groups (Pipho 1978). The continuing decline of scores on national tests of scholastic aptitude was the most visible indicator of trouble, although such tests as the SAT and the ACT are not functional literacy tests but are meant as predictors of success during the freshman year in college. Along with the results of the National Assessment of Educational Progress, the declining scores provided a rallying point for those who wanted to do something about the current state of public education. The early involvement of lawmakers rather than educators, however, indicated the political potency of the issue. Second, the movement has been a local grass roots phenomenon, producing state laws and local standards rather than a response to pressure from the federal government (Neill 1978, p. 42). The movement has been characterized by innovation, experimentation, and diversity, backed by strong political support (Lerner 1981, p. 1064). Third, the aims of efforts at minimum competence testing have been as limited educationally as they have been widespread geographically. It is an indication of the recent decline in American education that massive public pressure and legislative action have been mobilized to ensure that high school graduates are functionally literate and in command of fundamental life skills.

What Is Basic?

Even within a relatively homogeneous school population, students have a wide range of educational and life experiences, native ability, interests, and aspirations. Throughout the 1960s, schools increasingly responded to the needs of particular groups of students and gave greater autonomy to students in choosing programs and courses. The trend to minimum competence is an attempt to identify what skills are needed by *all* students to function effectively in society—the lowest common denominator of survival skills. They include such skills as being responsible for routine and personal affairs at home and at work, communicating with other people, pursuing further formal or self-directed education, getting and holding a job, and being a responsible citizen (American Friends 1979, p. 2). The Oregon State Board of Education designed its competence-based program and high school graduation requirements around skills "to function in six life roles: individual, learner, producer, citizen, consumer, and family member" (Neill 1978, p. 43). Each of these areas embodies a variety of skills and areas of knowledge.

Pressure for minimum competence testing has forced school officials to focus on what is being taught and how competence is measured. Underpinning this pressure is a

The impetus for minimum competence testing sets it apart from . . . educational innovations of the last two decades.

fairly general consensus that reading, math, and writing skills are fundamental both to functioning in adult society and in pursuing further education, either vocational or academic. Lerner, for example, describes requirements for functional literacy and numeracy not as arbitrary blocks to progress but intrinsic necessities for most types of skilled work in any advanced industrial society today (1981, p. 1060). General agreement on the need to return to the three Rs, however, does not make clear what degree of mastery of each skill is sufficient or how traditional school skills mesh with life or job skills (Pipho 1978, p. 586).

Minimum competence tests are *criterion-referenced*, which means that the student's performance is measured by his mastery of certain skills or subject matter rather than by comparison with the performance of other students taking the same or comparable tests. Commentators stress the need for policy makers to consider in advance the range of competencies and the variety of contexts in which they might be measured. Brickell posited five choices: basic skills (such as reading, writing, arithmetic), school subjects (such as art, business, English), life areas (citizenship, work, family), basic skills applied in school subjects, and basic skills applied in life areas (1978, p. 589; American Friends 1979, p. 28). Deciding on one or another of these choices has consequences for curriculum and for evaluation. The National Commission on Excellence in Education, for example, stressed high standards for school subjects but criticized such life skill courses as "bachelor living" (1983, p. 19).

Brickell also proposed a variety of schemes for measuring competence. They include actual or simulated performances, school projects, and traditional paper and pencil tests (1978). While an actual or simulated performance might be most appropriate for testing life skills, its use is generally limited to individual classrooms. States and local school districts almost universally choose paper and pencil tests because they are cheap and easy to administer and grade. As critics point out, the disadvantages of such tests include their inability to predict future success and their failure to measure personal qualities like energy, integrity, or creativity.

The definition of minimum competence testing used at hearings in 1980 sponsored by the National Institute of

Education (NIE) reflects possible variations in the focus
and use of tests:

> *Minimum competency testing refers to programs
> mandated by a state or local body which have the
> following characteristics: (1) all or almost all students of
> designated grades are required to take paper-and-pencil
> tests designed to measure basic academic skills, life or
> survival skills, or functional literacy; (2) a passing score
> or standard for acceptable levels of student performance
> has been established; and (3) test results may be used to
> certify students for grade promotion, graduation, or
> diploma award; to classify students for or to place
> students in remedial or other special services; to allocate
> compensatory funds to districts; to evaluate or to certify
> schools or school districts; or to evaluate teachers*
> (Thurston and House 1981, p. 87).

Experience now suggests several decision points with
significant impact on the successful implementation of
minimum competence testing: the allocation of responsibility, frequency and appropriateness of tests, provision of
support services, and protection of special groups.

Local Input
The implementation of minimum competence testing has
broadly retained the traditional allocation of responsibilities between state and local government (Haney and
Madaus 1978, p. 476; Whitla 1982, p. 30). Most commonly,
state officials set standards for students' performance at
key transition points—for example, from 8th grade into
high school and at high school graduation. Local officials
retain control over curricular matters and decisions about
grade-to-grade promotions. California's state legislature,
for example, required the adoption of proficiency standards
for reading, writing, and computation in effect for the
graduation of students in 1980 but left the adoption of
specific standards up to local school boards. The law's
author, Gary K. Hart, a former high school teacher,
stressed the importance of school districts' "retaining local
ownership of the standard setting process" (Hart 1978,
p. 593). Locally formulated standards ensure stronger
public support, tie what is tested more closely to what is

taught, allow for diversity and flexibility, and ease the reevaluation of goals, curricula, and remedial strategies. The California law also provided that the State Board of Education could supply performance indicators and examples of minimum standards to assist local school districts in formulating standards and test instruments (Pipho 1981, p. 2).

Periodic Reassessment
Opponents of minimum competence tests warn against basing an important educational passage—graduation, for example—on a single test score. The trend therefore is toward more frequent and earlier administration of tests. California, which originally called for testing once between grades 7 and 9 and twice between grades 10 and 11, added a requirement for testing once between grades 4 and 6 (Hart 1978, p. 593; Pipho 1981, p. 2). In the District of Columbia, students must complete 70 percent of required proficiencies at the end of each semester, a policy now being questioned by school officials (White 1983). In general, the more serious the consequences for failing to demonstrate the required basic skills, the more lead time is necessary to publicize standards and bring students up to par (Popham 1981, p. 90).

Appropriate Tests
To maximize the usefulness of minimum competence tests for students and school systems, testing must be related directly to the school district's instructional program. The minimally acceptable score should be determined in a systematic manner based on research (Popham 1981, p. 90) with careful advance planning. This method may require pilot tests to determine how many students pass and a determination of how many students a state or school district could afford not to promote or graduate if remedial programs failed (Brickell 1978, p. 591). Experience or political pressure may dictate a reexamination of the passing score. In Maryland, for example, officials began to question a passing score of 80 on a state mathematics proficiency exam when one-third of the students in Montgomery County failed although the same group averaged in the 78th percentile on the California Test of Basic Skills

(Walsh 1983). In Prince Georges County, nearly three-quarters of 9th graders failed (Wynter 1983b).

Support Services

Successful efforts to achieve minimum competence involve teachers, students, and parents. Staff support and development are essential. The program of measurement-driven instruction in Detroit, for example, included written program manuals for teachers and audiocassettes describing the major competencies and instructional strategies, workshops, and practice exercises (Popham and Rankin 1980). Even where teachers have been adequately trained and adequate time allowed, some students will not demonstrate the required mastery of basic skills. Unless remedial programs are in place, repeated administrations of the test may not improve a student's performance. Parents must also be notified if their child is experiencing difficulties. In some communities, handbooks have been prepared to help parents understand the various types of tests and to interpret what test scores mean (American Friends 1979; D.C. Citizens 1978). Popular magazines are frequently a source of information (Comer 1983).

While commentators and practitioners have thus identified a number of elements essential to a well-planned program of competence testing, opponents have focused on "serious, unintended negative consequences associated with the well-intentioned use" of such programs (Madaus 1981, p. 92). Ironically, they may affect both the most academically able as well as the most educationally disadvantaged students.

Dangers of a Single Standard

Although a major trend in education over recent decades has been to recognize individual differences in capacity and learning style, the minimum competence test institutes a single standard of success, which for able students may mean a diminution of quality. Courses aimed at the minimum standard may neglect students who can do far more. High schools need to prepare students who can not only balance a checkbook but also reason and compute in highly sophisticated ways (Bailey 1981). Teachers may focus on repetition and drill to prepare students for the test at the expense of other, more creative methods of learning the same material. A return to old standards need not mean a return to old methods. The "rising tide of mediocrity" deplored by the National Commission on Excellence in Education (1983, p. 5) will not be stemmed by an increase in functional literacy alone.

The potential danger of overconcentration on basic skills was suggested by an analysis of the results of the National Assessment of Educational Progress released in early 1983. Some observers have likened the National Assessment to the types and level of skills measured by minimum competence tests (Farr and Olshavsky 1980, pp. 528–29). The study compared reading, math, and science scores registered by groups of 9-, 13-, and 17-year-olds during the 1970s. It found that low-achieving students, whose scores fell in the bottom quarter, had made major gains, particularly in reading, but that high-achieving students, with scores in the top quarter, had lost ground, especially in math and science. Although white students had higher scores overall, black students in both high and low achievement groups had scored greater gains. Black low achievers scored significant gains in reading and math and held their own in science. Experts who studied the results attributed the gains to federally funded compensatory education programs and to increased local emphasis on basic skills. Noting the declining performance of high-achieving students, however, they called for a reexamination of the back-to-basics philosophy. "Lower order, so-called basic skills are not necessarily the building blocks essential to acquiring higher order cognitive skills such as problem-solving, analyzing, and synthesizing" (Peterson 1983). Farr and Olshavsky agree. They concluded that evidence from the National Assessment of Educational Progress shows a high level of basic literacy.

> If a state or school system wants to improve literacy levels, it does not seem that greater emphasis is needed on lower-level reading achievement. What is needed is increased emphasis on higher level reading/thinking skills (1980, p. 530).

Using earlier data from the National Assessment, however, Lerner found minimum competence testing justified by unacceptably high levels of functional illiteracy and semiilliteracy (1981).

Misuse of Tests

As with standardized aptitude tests, the major problem
with minimum competence testing is not the test itself but
how the results are used. Thus, the same test can be
harmful or useful. The potential for harm must be mini-
mized with informed test makers, test takers, and test
users. Participants in the NIE debate on competence
testing agreed at the outset that the results not be used to
allocate funds or evaluate teachers (Thurston and House
1981, p. 87). The National Education Association has gone
on record against combining individual scores to evaluate
teachers' performance, determine promotions, or compare
schools (1982, p. 51).

In states where failure to meet certain standards can
mean loss of a high school diploma, handicapped and
learning disabled students may be unfairly affected
(Madaus 1981, p. 94). Commentators and practitioners are
increasingly sensitive to this issue (*Higher Education
Daily* 1982d), with the result that alternative standards are
being developed. In some states, laws governing minimum
competence testing provide specifically for handicapped
students. Illinois law, for example, requires that minimum
competence testing not be used to prohibit the graduation
of a handicapped student if failure is related to the handi-
capping condition (Pipho 1981, p. 5). Indiana law excludes
students whose dominant language is not English, grants
discretionary participation to the mentally handicapped,
learning disabled, and emotionally disturbed, and requires
that handicapped students be tested in a manner appropriate to their needs (Pipho 1981, p. 6). In contrast, North
Carolina requires that handicapped students take the state
competence test (Pipho 1981, p. 13).

The disproportionate adverse impact of minimum
competence testing on minority students has raised serious
questions of equity (NAACP 1983a). Test designers are
cautioned to guard against cultural bias in test questions.
Detroit's program of measurement-driven instruction, for
example, involves a team of black test reviewers to detect
and eliminate items that might be biased against minority
or economically disadvantaged students (Popham and
Rankin 1980, p. 208). Opponents of testing, however,
contend that such bias often creeps in undetected and that
the test as a whole rather than individual items discrimi-

nates against minority students. Minority observers point to situations where the phase-in period is too short to compensate for previously inadequate educational opportunities (Down 1979; NAACP 1983a, p. 1). Lewis distinguishes between competence-based education and minimum competence testing. He contends that competence-based education provides a way to structure educational goals around outcomes, diagnose individual needs, individualize instruction, and provide remedial help. In contrast, minimum competence testing may lead to resegregation or the maintenance of an inadequate status quo (Lewis 1979).

A major controversy surrounds the use of minimum competence tests as a criterion for receiving a high school diploma. Both the NAACP and the National Education Association oppose such tests as a requirement for graduation (NAACP 1983a, p. 1; NEA 1982, p. 51). In the case of *Debra P.* v. *Turlington,* black students challenged Florida's use of minimum competence testing as a condition of high school graduation.* The suit promises to be an important precedent for other states considering such a requirement.

Florida was the first state to require passage of a statewide functional literacy test as a requirement of high school graduation (Fisher 1978; Glass 1978). The Educational Accountability Act, passed in 1976 and amended in 1978, requires completion of a minimum number of course credits prescribed by local school boards, mastery of basic skills, and demonstration of functional literacy. The law provides that students who complete the credits but fail the examination receive a certificate of completion rather than a high school diploma. It also requires periodic retesting and locally developed programs of remediation. Although state education officials had been working on statewide objectives for basic skills, trial testimony indicated the crucial role of the state legislature in redirecting this effort to functional objectives. Plaintiffs noted both the scanty legislative language and the strict time limitations. The State Board approved state minimum student performance standards, drafted by the State Department of Education, in April 1977. Results of the October 1977 testing were

* *Debra P.* v. *Turlington,* 474 F. Supp. 244 (M.D. Fla. 1979); *modified,* 644 F. 2d 397 (5th Cir. 1981); rehearing denied. 654 F. 2d 1079 (5th Cir. 1981).

announced in December 1977 so that students retaking the test for the third time in April 1979 had only 13 months of instructional time in which to prepare.

As state officials had anticipated during development of the test, the failure rate of black students was several times that of white students. For purposes of scoring, the test was divided into two parts—communications (geared to a 7th grade level) and math (geared to an 8th grade level)—with a 70 percent passing score required on each. A student passing one part did not have to retake it. On the first administration, 36 percent of all students failed one or both parts, but 78 percent of black students failed one or both parts compared to 25 percent of white students. Further, 26 percent of black students failed communications compared to 3 percent of whites, and 77 percent of black students failed math compared to 24 percent of whites. On subsequent administrations, the performance of both blacks and whites improved, but black students still failed at a disproportionately high rate.

Black students sought to enjoin the state of Florida and its education commissioner from instituting the functional literacy test as a condition of graduation from high school. In July 1979, a federal district court judge, citing the vestigial effects of legally imposed segregation on black students still in Florida schools, delayed for four years the literacy test as a requirement to receive a high school diploma (for a critical view of Judge Carr's initial decision, see Lerner 1980, pp. 144–47). In 1981, a federal circuit court of appeals modified that ruling. The court looked not only at the racially discriminatory impact of previous schooling but also at the relationship between what was tested on the statewide examination and what was taught in Florida schools. The court held that the use of the test would be prohibited even beyond the four-year postponement "if the test is found to be invalid for the reason that it tests matters outside the curriculum." Such invalidity would violate the Equal Protection Clause of the 14th Amendment. In May 1983, Judge Carr upheld the validity of the test and ruled that Florida may deny high school diplomas and grant only certificates of completion to seniors failing to pass it. He also refused to delay implementation of his ruling while the case is again appealed. Of the 1,300 students denied diplomas, two-thirds were black, although only one-fifth of Florida's student population is black (*Washington Post* 1983e).

The case of *Debra P.* v. *Turlington* focused on the end point of a process beginning in the early grades. The Educational Accountability Act provides for testing the basic skills of all students in grades 3, 5, 8, and 11 with promotion delayed until a student masters the requisite skills. State officials set minimum standards for each grade in reading, writing, and math. Local districts are responsible for establishing pupil progression programs compatible with the standards. State funding for remedial programs helps local districts bring students' performance up to minimum standards. Students, both black and white, now entering Florida schools will take the functional literacy test for high school graduation after years of exposure to minimum basic skills and practice with competence testing. Experience has already shown that performance improves on retesting. With sufficient lead time, clearly stated standards, adequate diagnostic and remedial programs, officials may expect the failure rate of both races to decline and the performance levels of all students to rise.

In Georgia, a suit against a county school district raised on the local level many of the issues that *Debra P.* v. *Turlington* raised on the state level (Flygare 1981). Plaintiffs in *Anderson* v. *Banks* objected to the requirement that graduating seniors score 9.0 in both reading and math on the California Achievement Test, a national norm-referenced examination on which a 9.0 score indicates achievement at the level of the average beginning 9th grader. Of 48 students who failed to score 9.0 in three years of testing, 33 were black. Test results showed that the average score rose and the number of students failing each time dropped significantly. In a ruling similar to that in the Florida case, a federal district judge held that the diploma sanction could not be imposed until 1983, when graduating students would not have been disadvantaged by the district's previously segregated school system. The court found that the lead time allowed and the remedial courses provided were sufficient. Nevertheless, it held that the California test could not be used unless district officials could establish that the test items matched the curriculum taught in Tattnall County schools. Presumably, for black students in states or school districts without a history of racial segregation but where black students failed competence tests in disproportionate numbers, this argument might be sufficient to block the use of certain types of tests.

The experience to date with minimum competence testing seems to confirm fundamental principles for the successful implementation of any major educational program or change. These principles include the importance of local input in planning and implementation, adequate lead time and public information, periodic evaluation, support services for staff and students, appropriate links between the perceived problem and the proffered solution, and sensitivity to the needs of special students. The trend of recent court decisions is to uphold diploma sanctions when protective measures for minority students are in place.

The goal of the movement toward minimum competence testing—to increase the number and proportion of high school graduates who are functionally literate—is worthy but apparently anachronistic at a time when more than half of all high school graduates go on to higher education. It is one measure of decline that efforts to achieve 9th grade competence in reading, math, and writing have stolen center stage from the goal of universal access to postsecondary education. Just as many of the benefits of minimum competence testing have been realized, so too have some of its potential dangers. The application of a single minimum standard to a diverse high school population threatens the advanced skills of high achievers (*Chronicle* 1983f, p. 13; National Commission 1983, p. 13; Peterson 1983; Southern Regional Education Board 1982a, p. 1). It constitutes only one step in the long continuum of preparation from elementary school through college.

Educators, legislators, state and local officials, and the public are increasingly aware of the connections between elementary and secondary school programs and students' performance in college. Preparation for college involves efforts to determine what high school courses are necessary for the college-bound student, what academic skills are necessary to handle college-level work, and who is responsible for defining, implementing, and funding changes in requirements. Poor preparation is affecting students of all levels of ability. Cooperative efforts are now underway—but more are necessary—to improve preparatory work at the high school level and to ease the transition to college (Watkins 1983a).

Course Work
Recent reports indicate a renewed appreciation of the relationship between curricula and academic standards. In a presentation to the College Board, Kirst outlined the following trends:

- a serious decline in the frequency of students' electing more advanced courses
- reduced content and expectation in advanced courses
- weakened requirements for graduation
- use of less challenging texts (1981, p. 5).

The National Commission on Excellence in Education reported that secondary school curricula have lost coherence and that they are "homogenized, diluted, and diffused to the point that they no longer have a central purpose" (*Chronicle* 1983f, p. 12; National Commission 1983, p. 18). Students have strayed from vocational and college preparatory programs into a "general track," with fewer students taking more advanced, rigorous academic courses and more students earning credits in health, physical education, remedial training, and personal service and development (*Chronicle* 1983f, p. 13; National Commission 1983, p. 19). The commission found that in 13 states, requirements for graduation could be satisfied with more than 50 percent elective units. It has also become increasingly difficult to gauge the academic rigor of a course. The proliferation of courses offered in response to earlier demands for "relevance" transformed the educational landscape, making it nearly impossible to compare offerings at different schools (Kirst 1981, p. 17). Similarly, the trend to higher grades has made it harder to compare students on the basis of grade point average.

Writing in 1962 about the relationship between school curricula and college, Otto Kraushaar envisioned a steady improvement in precollegiate preparation.

Recent reports indicate a renewed appreciation of the relationship between curricula and academic standards.

Suppose that within the next two decades good college matriculants were to arrive equipped with ten years of foreign language, with training in mathematics at least through calculus, proficient in written and spoken English, with a solid foundation in biological and physical science, and a good general education in the arts. What would the colleges make of this millenium? (Menacker 1975, p. 50).

Instead, colleges have increasingly assumed the burden of remedial work to bring students up to college level (Feinberg 1982a). Confronted with poorly trained students and with diminishing resources to fulfill traditional institutional missions, college officials are seeking to shift remedial responsibilities back to the secondary schools (Southern Regional Education Board 1982a).

College readiness can be gauged by the completion of specified courses or the mastery of specific skills. Relying on the 1980 survey of state requirements for high school diplomas, the National Commission on Excellence in Education found that only eight states required that high schools offer foreign language courses but none required that students take them. Thirty-five states required only one year of math; 36 required only one year of science (*Chronicle* 1983f, p. 13; National Commission 1983, p. 20). The National Association of Secondary School Principals noted, however, that the trend was to greater concern for students' competence in a variety of subject areas as well as basic skills (Parrish 1980).

The National Commission on Excellence in Education called for strengthened state and local requirements for high school graduation for *all* students. It described the "five new basics" as the minimum foundation courses: four years of English, three years of mathematics, three years of science, three years of social studies, and one-half year of computer science. It recommended two years of foreign language study for college-bound students and urged that foreign language study begin at the elementary school level (*Chronicle* 1983f, p. 14; National Commission 1983, p. 24). The President's Commission on Foreign Languages and International Studies (1979) and the Twentieth Century Fund (*Chronicle* 1983g) made similar recommendations. The College Board's Project EQuality has identified and described in detail six subject matter areas deemed the basic academic curriculum. Complementing the project's basic academic competencies, which transcend particular disciplines, they include English, mathematics, foreign or second language, history and social science, natural science, and the performing arts (*Chronicle* 1983i; College Board 1983, pp. 13–30; Watkins 1983e).

State and Local Action
Action on the part of both states and local school districts is essential to the process of enhancing the quality of preparation for higher education. Part of the difficulty comes from joint responsibility and fragmented authority. The role of states in setting requirements for graduation from high school varies dramatically across the country. At one end of the spectrum, a state may leave the matter largely up to local school authorities. Michigan, for example, does not even specify units for high school graduation

and requires only a single semester course in civics. In such a system, school districts may rely on the standards of school accrediting associations (Parrish 1980, p. 11). At the other end of the spectrum, a state board may set requirements for total units, course distribution for graduation, and different standards for state and local diplomas. In New York, the course distributions for a local and a Regents diploma are the same, but a student earning a Regents diploma must complete 18 rather than 16 units and must pass statewide Regents examinations in specified subjects.

The trend at the state level is to more specific requirements for high school graduation covering not only course distribution but also refining the types of courses that will fulfill the requirements in various fields. Activities like working on the school paper are returning to their status of extracurricular activities. States are increasing the number of units required for high school graduation and are differentiating more sharply the graduation requirements for students in college preparatory courses. In 1983, Virginia's Superintendent of Public Instruction called for completion of 22 units by college-bound students, including three years of study in mathematics, science, and foreign language (Southern Regional Education Board 1983, p. 3).

While state boards may set requirements for units or distribution or establish standards for minimum performance, local school districts retain major areas of authority. In states like Michigan, nearly the entire responsibility for setting standards falls at the local level. More frequently, however, local officials establish higher standards than the minimal ones set at the state level. In Maryland, for example, the state requires 20 units for graduation (Parrish 1980, p. 2), but county school boards may add to the minimums in various subject areas. The Prince Georges County Board of Education voted to require additional math and social studies courses for a total of 14 units in academic subjects (Wynter 1983a). Such changes are being instituted not only to better prepare graduates for college or the changing job market but also to force seniors back into classrooms during their final year in high school.

Changes in course requirements may not necessarily improve students' performance. Menacker, for example, argues that subjects in high school are not as accurate a predictor of success in college as high school grade point average combined with scores on standardized tests. "Specific subjects as factors of the predictive formula do not improve accuracy" (1975, p. 11). The College Board reports that students' achievement scores in mathematics continued to drop in the period from 1977 to 1981 even though students reported taking additional high school courses in mathematics and physical sciences (1982b, p. 7). A student is unlikely to learn French or chemistry without taking a French or chemistry class, however. The coincidence of increasingly diffuse academic programs with manifest indicators of declines in all areas suggests the need to return coherence to requirements in secondary schools.

The adequacy of preparation for college may be gauged not only by completion of requisite courses but also by mastery of skills essential for college-level work. "Lists of required courses or hours in English or mathematics offer only a crude quantification of what colleges look for in the way of academic preparation. Beyond credit units there are invisible expectations" (College Board 1982a, p. 1). In response to the decline in academic achievement among high school students, the College Board has undertaken Project EQuality to strengthen the quality of secondary education and to ensure equality of opportunity for postsecondary education for all students. The project is significant for its long-term commitment—it is planned as a 10-year effort—and for combining the major aspects of minority access and academic excellence. It has sought to relate learning skills and subject mastery as interdependent aspects of preparation for college.

As a first step, Project EQuality helped formulate the "basic academic competencies," which are a functionally organized description of what academic preparation for college in the 1980s should be. They transcend particular subject areas and are defined as "developed abilities which come from learning and intellectual discourse, related to and interdependent with basic subject matter and without which knowledge of other disciplines would be unattainable" (College Board 1981a, p. 1; College Board 1983, pp. 7–10). These competencies include reading competencies, writing competencies, speaking and listening competencies, mathematical competencies, reasoning competencies, and studying competencies. They are based on discussions with school and college teachers and administrators. State education policy makers are being encouraged to consider them when formulating standards for graduation from high school and requirements for admission to college.

Early signs indicate a favorable reception by a variety of groups. The competencies have been accepted or endorsed in part by the American Federation of Teachers and the state higher education office or education agency in California, Idaho, Kentucky, and Tennessee. Elsewhere, Project EQuality is providing a way for high schools and colleges to work together to improve the academic preparation of high school students (Watkins 1983e, p. 14). In California, public college and university professors adopted competencies in English, math, and reading, reflecting Project EQuality's concerns, which they expect of incoming students (College Board 1982b; McCurdy 1981). Endorsed by the academic senates of California's public institutions, the statement concludes that requiring completion of academic courses in high school is not sufficient preparation. It calls instead for "clear communication of the nature of these requisite skills to all high school juniors and seniors."

The early success of Project EQuality is an important reminder of the value of dialogue between parts of the academic community. Consideration of the basic academic competencies by professors, academic unions, governors, legislators, school boards, school teachers, teachers colleges, and businessmen may redirect efforts to allocate blame for declining education indicators. In particular, a return to quality and coherence in education will require cooperation between state and local officials and between college and high school teachers and administrators.

Institutional Cooperation
Cooperation between high schools and colleges will be one of the most important developments in the 1980s. Paradoxically, relations between high schools and colleges deteriorated in both boom times and hard times for education. In the early 1960s, when well-prepared graduates competed for limited spaces at selective colleges, rapport broke down between high school counselors and college admissions personnel (Sjogren 1982a, p. 15). Rising standards for

admission pressured developers of high school curricula to offer the requisite courses in the "basic five" subject areas. In the 1970s, however, colleges tended to relax their own degree requirements while maintaining rigid entrance standards. High schools again responded, offering more numerous, more diverse, and often less rigorous courses and reducing requirements for foreign language study, mathematics, and laboratory science courses (Casteen 1982; Maeroff 1983, p. 2; Sjogren 1982a, p. 17). In each case, changes in standards at the high school level were a reaction to perceived changes at the college level rather than the result of consultation and consideration between educators or administrators from the two sectors. Left on their own, many students failed to take courses that would best prepare them to get the most out of college. "In its peculiar way, justice prevailed, with institutions of higher education being forced to mount remedial courses for these same students" (Maeroff 1983, p. 3).

The current reflection on students' performance and educational excellence is in some respects a rediscovery of old verities, seen through the prism of experience of the 1970s. While internal standards of performance are becoming more rigorous at both the high school and college levels, lines between the two are becoming more flexible. Both institutional and attitudinal barriers will need to fall.

The basic answer to both problems of evaluating the preparation of high school graduates for college and integrating secondary education experience with college education lies in improved articulation between school and college (Menacker 1975, p. 50).

The intensified interest in the American high school (Watkins 1982b) is one indicator that links between institutional levels are already being renewed. As part of the work of the Carnegie Foundation for the Advancement of Teaching on the American high school, Ernest L. Boyer proposed principles on which to base cooperative efforts between high schools and colleges:

- to agree that schools and colleges have common problems

- to overcome the traditional pecking order in which higher education acts and high schools react
- to focus collaborative efforts sharply
- to concentrate on action and not on bureaucracy and budgets
- to recognize and reward participants in collaborative projects (American Association for Higher Education 1981, pp. 1–3; Maeroff 1983, pp. 1–6).

Other groups seeking to raise academic standards have also stressed the need for cooperative planning and joint action. The Task Force on Higher Education and the schools of the Southern Regional Education Board (SREB) recommended that states establish joint committees with representatives from state boards of education and higher education "to consider concerted action to establish and raise standards both for the high school curriculum and for the general education component of higher education" (SREB Task Force 1981, p. 19).

Although interest has been renewed in collaborative efforts to improve the quality of secondary school preparation for higher education, some such programs are well established. The National Commission on Excellence in Education acknowledged the existence of meritorious schools and programs but concluded that ". . . their very distinction stands out against a vast mass shaped by tensions and pressures that inhibit systematic academic and vocational achievement for the majority of students" (*Chronicle* 1983f, p. 12; National Commission 1983, p. 14). In a study for the Carnegie Foundation, on the other hand, Maeroff reported on a number of successful projects representing a "dramatic upsurge in collaboration. Colleges and schools have come together to accomplish clear, explicit goals, objectives that should be pursued by every institution in every state" (1983, p. viii).

Collaborative efforts to improve the quality of preparation for college and to ease the transition between high school and college work involve variations on three major components of education: time, course content, and institutional organization. Examples of each show ways in which flexibility and innovation combined with high academic standards may produce major advances.

Time

While concern is widespread that time in school be increased and used more efficiently, support is also growing for breaking the academic lockstep from kindergarten to grade 12 and on to higher education.

> *Placement and grouping of students, as well as promotion and graduation policies, should be guided by the academic progress of students and their instructional needs, rather than by rigid adherence to age (Chronicle 1983f, p. 14; National Commission 1983, p. 30).*

Similarly, the report for the Carnegie Foundation questions the sanctity of the traditional four years in high school followed by four years of college. Relaxed standards for required courses in some states have already created a vestigial senior year. The report urges that "colleges and schools . . . work together to overcome the tyranny of time. Students should be free to move at their own pace, more flexibly to make the transition from school to college" (Maeroff 1983, p. viii).

Some states have provided ways for students to graduate from high school early. California, which pioneered the "early-out" test in 1975, permits students aged 16 (or younger if they have completed or are about to complete 10th grade) to leave school immediately upon passing a state proficiency examination covering basic skills. They include communications skills (reading, writing, and language) and problem-solving skills (arithmetic reasoning, computation, interpretation of graphs and scales) (see Neill 1978, pp. 49–50, for examples of typical items). The test was developed by the California State Department of Education, which drew on a variety of sources, including the National Assessment of Educational Progress and commercial standardized tests. The test takes four hours to complete, and a passing score is set at the average level of a second semester California high school senior. It requires short answers and an essay and involves little recall of facts. Those who pass receive a certificate of proficiency, which is legally equivalent to a high school diploma, and are eligible to enter the state's college system. The certificate may not be substituted for a transcript of course work or standardized test scores, however.

Since 1977, Florida has offered 16-year-olds the option

of leaving school before graduation (Neill 1978, p. 52). Its program differs from California's in several respects. The test is the high school equivalency test, the GED (General Education Development), covering reading, writing, math, social studies, and science. It takes 10 hours to complete and is geared to a 9th grade reading level. Students taking the test must have their parents' permission and must discuss their career or academic plans with a school official. Students who pass must leave school and may not return. (In California, in contrast, a passing student need not leave high school, and those who do may return.)

The value of the early-out system is the flexibility it gives to students in designating their high school program and the apparent financial savings to the state. The benefits in terms of quality are not so clear. An able student may fulfill the requirements but lack depth; high schools may be tempted to pass above-average students on to state colleges and concentrate on getting low achievers through minimum competence tests; state colleges may be ill prepared to handle the academic, social, and psychological needs of a younger clientele; 16-year-olds who do not wish to continue their education may have difficulty securing employment. As a corollary, many states that initially considered a test for leaving early did not adopt one (Neill 1978, p. 50).

. . . support is . . . growing for breaking the academic lockstep from kindergarten to . . . higher education.

Course content

An alternative to sending students to college at an earlier age is incorporating college-level courses in the high school curriculum. The venerability of the 30-year-old Advanced Placement (AP) Program of the College Board is testimony to the program's inherent worthiness as well as to a possible lapse in the imaginative powers of high school/college collaborators. From 1973 to 1981, a period now seen as one of significant academic decline, the number of students participating in the AP program increased 152 percent (Southern Regional Education Board 1982c, p. 2). Taught by high school teachers in high school settings, students in AP courses are tested and scored by the Educational Testing Service. Upon entering college, these students may receive academic credit and/or automatic placement in a higher-level course on the basis of their AP examination. In 1982, over 140,000 students at 5,525 high schools nationwide took AP examinations (Maeroff 1983, p. 17).

Problems of access may affect able students as well as academically disadvantaged ones. The Southern Regional Education Board has expressed concern that southern states have not participated in the AP program to the same extent that the rest of the nation has. In 1981, only 17 percent of the high schools in SREB states participated in the program, compared to 22 percent nationally. Only Maryland, South Carolina, and Virginia exceeded the national ratio. Furthermore, the region suffered a net loss of AP students who went to colleges outside the region. Maryland and Florida were particularly affected by this outward migration, while North Carolina showed substantial gains (Southern Regional Education Board 1982c, p. 4), suggesting that institutions like the University of Maryland, which are trying to attract outstanding students from other states, should increase their efforts to retain outstanding natives (Muscatine 1983).

Because college-level courses offered in high schools are by their very nature aimed at the most able students, they are also subject to charges of elitism. Because of problems in the past with students "tracked" along racial or economic lines, schools that offer enriched or accelerated courses or special academic high schools must safeguard against unfairness in their procedures for selecting students (Southern Regional Education Board 1982a, p. 6). In some schools, labeling students as "gifted and talented" has become a problem comparable to labeling them as handicapped or otherwise disadvantaged (Zibart 1983). Most observers consider that the presence of an AP or gifted and talented program in a school invigorates the entire curriculum. Nevertheless, the dangers of tracking, inflexible admissions to special programs, and labeling need to be kept in mind.

Special opportunities for high school teachers provide another means to improve the quality of academic preparation in high school. Project Advance, run by Syracuse University, is heralded by virtually every reporter (American Association for Higher Education 1981, p. 6; Maeroff 1983, pp. 20–21; National Commission 1982a, p. 2; Southern Regional Education Board 1982c, p. 1). The project involves courses taught for college credit in 75 high schools in four states by teachers who participate in special summer workshops and who use the same materials in class as freshmen at Syracuse in comparable introductory courses. Syracuse gives credit to participating students who later enroll there or sends a transcript to another institution. Ninety-eight percent of the students participating attended college and achieved higher grades, completed degrees, and pursued graduate studies at significantly higher rates than the national averages. Only a small percentage (12 percent) completed requirements for a degree in less than the usual time. An important aspect of the project is the status conferred on participating faculty: They are called "adjunct instructors" and receive tuition benefits for courses at Syracuse (National Commission 1982a, p. 2).

Programs conducted on college campuses for high school students are another popular variety of collaborative projects. The Accelerated High School Student Program at the University of California at Berkeley is one example. High school seniors may take up to two courses per quarter, up to ten academic credits, in the same classes and according to the same standards as regularly enrolled students (Maeroff 1983, p. 19). According to the Carnegie Council on Policy Studies in Higher Education, nearly 40 percent of the nation's community colleges and 16 percent of liberal arts colleges allow participation of high school students in courses on campus. But much of this participation is on an ad hoc basis with little coordination between institutions as to class schedules or academic calendars. Speaking at the symposium held in honor of the tenth anniversary of the Fund for the Improvement of Postsecondary Education, Stephen Horn urged that educators at different institutions, high schools, community colleges, and four-year colleges in the same geographic location make a great effort to know each other as a first step toward working together in a more organized way.*

Institutional organization
Some states and school districts are moving beyond enriched curricula and joint high school/college programs.

*Remarks at the public forum on "Priorities for Improvement," Washington, D.C., 27 March 1983.

New institutional models are providing alternatives to the traditional high school and to the customary time sequence. Southern states in particular are moving to residential high schools for gifted students. For example, a special school for math and science is located in North Carolina, a residential school for gifted and talented 11th and 12th grade students is located on the campus of Northwestern State University in Louisiana, and a residential school for gifted students is proposed for Virginia (Southern Regional Education Board 1982b, p. 5).

Integrated or time-condensed programs provide an alternative to the typical high school organization. Both Middle College of LaGuardia Community College in Long Island City and Matteo Ricci College in Seattle, Washington, were established in the mid-1970s to function as both high school and college. Students can complete high school requirements and earn concurrent credit for college work (American Association for Higher Education 1981, p. 7; Maeroff 1983, pp. 50–53). At Matteo Ricci, students enter at grade 9 and can complete a B.A. degree by grade 14. Curriculum, intended to eliminate duplication and fragmentation, is composed of three-year integrated courses in composition, aesthetic development, unified science, foreign language, mathematics, cultural studies, religious development, humanistic inquiry, and psychophysical development. According to the American College Testing Program Comprehensive Outcomes Measurement Project analysis (COMP), Matteo Ricci students perform at levels comparable to or higher than local and national control groups (Maeroff 1983, pp. 46–48; National Commission 1982a, pp. 2–3).

Middle College High School differs from the new state-supported schools for gifted and talented students in its appeal to a constituency of ethnic and academic diversity. It provides an important model for the academic preparation of minority students. Organizationally, Middle College benefits from its ties to the New York City Board of Education and the City College of New York. Its high school–age students benefit from the proximity of the community college and the motivational role of career education supervisors. Eighty-five percent of Middle College graduates go on to college (National Commission 1982a, p. 6).

Some programs, such as Project CHAMP at the University of Wisconsin–Parkside, are aimed specifically at increasing the motivation of underprepared and minority students. The staff of Project CHAMP encourage students to take more challenging courses and to consider appropriate career goals and postsecondary education. Summer workshops combine motivational strategies with emphasis on improving basic skills (National Commission 1982a, p. 5). Other programs have a particular academic emphasis. For example, the Select Program in Science and Engineering of the City College of New York involves 480 10th graders from 16 New York City high schools in Saturday morning programs centered around math and laboratory sciences. High school teachers also participate so that the momentum generated by the special program can be sustained in regular classroom work (Maeroff 1983, pp. 64–65; National Commission 1982a, p. 7).

These efforts coincide with the recommendations of the Commission on the Higher Education of Minorities concerning the precollegiate education of minorities:

- that secondary school counselors and teachers encourage minority students to enroll in college preparatory curricula and take courses in mathematics, languages, natural sciences, and social science;
- that secondary school teachers and administrators, working in collaboration with faculty from nearby colleges and universities, define intellectual competencies crucial to effective performance in college and develop tests to measure such competencies (Commission on the Higher Education of Minorities 1982, p. 25; Middleton 1982a, p. 10).

In the same vein, Maeroff recommends that institutions of higher education play a greater role in the elementary and secondary preparation of disadvantaged students. Early intervention measures might include summer programs, work with parents, campus visits, and academic advising (Maeroff 1983, p. xiii). In this area, as in others, sensitivity to the special needs of minority students can inform our view of what must be done generally to improve the responsiveness of schools and colleges to the needs of all students.

The role of tests in the transition of students from high school to college is highly visible but also widely misunderstood. In recent years, secondary schools, college admissions personnel, education researchers, minority groups, and taxpayers have all expressed concern about the use and misuse of standardized aptitude and achievement tests. Ironically, demands for minimum competence testing nationwide have coincided with calls for greater scrutiny and regulation of the testing industry and less reliance on test scores for decisions about admitting students to college (Brandt 1980, p. 657; National Research Council 1982, p. 7). Some have argued that competence testing is an inappropriate response to the decline in scholastic aptitude test scores (Farr and Olshavsky 1980). Both kinds of tests are important "education indicators." But they provide different information and suggest different concerns in restoring academic excellence.

Competence Testing versus Standardized Testing
Minimum competence tests and standardized aptitude and achievement tests measure different skills at different levels for different purposes. Competence tests evaluate basic academic or survival skills to determine a student's ability to function in adult society. The standards, set either at the state or local level, constitute a lowest common denominator for students' performance. Competence tests are criterion-referenced: the test is not meant to compare one student with another. It measures whether a student has mastered skills the school system is trying to teach. States prescribing minimum levels for competence testing generally have also formulated basic skills for each grade level, which school systems are expected to incorporate in their curricula. In legal challenges to minimum competence tests, the link between what is covered by the tests and what is actually taught in schools has become crucial to court approval of conditioning promotion or graduation on a passing score. The results of this type of testing can be used for diagnostic purposes, to identify particular weaknesses in a single student or to pinpoint areas where instructional methods might be improved. Feedback can be used immediately to improve performance.

Standardized tests for college admissions are prepared by testing companies like the Educational Testing Service or the American College Testing Program rather than by state or local educational personnel. They are designed to predict a student's ability to perform successfully during the first year of college. Standardized tests are administered nationwide. They are norm-referenced rather than criterion-referenced: a student's performance is measured against the performance of other students taking the same test or comparable tests given in the past. Aptitude tests do not measure a student's mastery of a given body of material. Questions are not derived from any particular course of study and coaching before the examination is supposed to be of minimal value in raising scores, although this is a matter of some debate (National Research Council 1982, pp. 196–98). Test results are often used to identify trends or to compare academic performance in different regions, of different ethnic minorities, or of the whole nation over time. They are generally not intended for diagnostic purposes and provide little particular information on deficient skills.

Achievement to Aptitude

Nationally standardized tests, such as the Scholastic Aptitude Test, were originally intended to give colleges a way to evaluate an applicant's potential beyond the often parochial or limited information available about his performance in high school. To a significant degree, this rationale still applies. The large number of high schools nationwide has traditionally made comparisons between academic programs difficult. More recently, problems of inflated grades and proliferating courses have added new complexities. Scores on standardized admissions tests are the lingua franca of college applicants amid a babble of conflicting, confusing, and subjective indicators.

The early history of educational testing indicates the link between aptitude, achievement, and precollegiate training. When only a small proportion of the population attended college, prospective students sat for examinations prepared by the college they hoped to attend. Helen Keller, for example, took examinations in German, French, English, Greek and Roman history, Latin, Greek, geometry, and algebra to qualify for admission to Radcliffe College in 1900 (Keller 1902, pp. 82–88). As the number of public high schools grew, the link between secondary preparation and

Minimum competence tests and standardized aptitude . . . tests measure different skills at different levels for different purposes.

collegiate requirements became attenuated. Students at a distance from the East Coast had no way to sit for examinations, promising candidates often lacked the traditional classical training, and college officials had insufficient information to evaluate unknown students from largely unknown schools.

The College Entrance Examination Board was formed in 1900 in response to these changes. The introduction of standard *achievement* tests provided a way to compare the academic preparation of students from many parts of the country. A small group of eastern colleges required applicants to take the College Board examinations or accepted them as a substitute for their own examinations. Most colleges, however, continued to rely on high school certification of applicants (National Research Council 1982, p. 92). As the number of qualified high school graduates increased, some colleges were faced with more qualified applicants than they could accept. Standard *aptitude* tests were introduced in 1926, signaling a further break from reliance on a prescribed set of precollegiate courses in favor of a more generalized display of verbal and mathematical ability. The Scholastic Aptitude Test was described as a test of a student's ability to learn rather than of mastery of information already learned. Over the following decade, the multiple choice aptitude test supplanted the essay-type achievement test as the instrument used to evaluate students seeking admission to the more selective eastern colleges (Resnick 1982, pp. 186–88). By the early 1940s, two other modifications in the testing program effectively established its present organization. First, at the urging of some of its members, the College Board administered the Scholastic Aptitude Test at locations across the country, thus expanding the pool from which promising students might be drawn. Second, achievement tests were recast into an objective format, eliminating for several decades the use of an essay examination as an admissions requirement (National Research Council 1982, pp. 92–93).

Standardization
The Scholastic Aptitude Test introduced standardization of several different sorts to admissions testing. Scores may be compared to those of students who took the examination at

the same time or who took other editions of the test in the past:

> *The purpose of the standardization process is to yield a measurement containing as little as possible of what we might call "irrelevant variance" and bias and to yield fair, objective scores on a scale with a common currency, one that will apply equally to all students everywhere who take the test. Ultimately, the goal of standardization is to achieve comparability—from student to student, from group to group, from one geographical area to another, and from one point in time to another* (Angoff 1981, pp. 17–18).

Test designers seek to ensure that different versions of the same test are comparable. By a process known as equating, psychometricians use statistical formulas to convert raw scores to a scaled score. A scaled score indicates a level of ability comparable to that represented by the same scaled score earned by a different student on another administration of the test. This process is meant to eliminate inevitable variations of difficulty from form to form on the same test. Scaled scores are not distributed on a curve whereby the proportion of high, medium, and low scores remains the same regardless of changes in the quality of students' performance. Grading on a curve would eliminate the comparability of scores over time and would make a student's score dependent in an inequitable way on the caliber of students tested at the same time (Angoff 1981, p. 19).

Until recently, both the Scholastic Aptitude Test and the American College Test Program examinations maintained scaled scores by equating new forms of the tests to previous forms. The score scales of the verbal and mathematical parts of the Scholastic Aptitude Test were established in 1941 with mean scores of 500 and standard deviations of 100 on a scale of 200 to 800. The score scales for the American College Testing Program examinations were established in 1959; they were based on the score system of the Iowa Test of Educational Development from which it evolved. The 25th, 50th, and 75th percentile ranks of high school seniors in 1973 fell at 11, 16, and 20 on a scale of 1 to 36 (National Research Council 1982, p. 48). Although the ACT is more closely tied to traditional subject areas (English, mathematics, social science, and natural science) than the SAT, a student's scores on the two tests tend to be closely related. Some colleges accept either score as part of the student's application (National Research Council 1982, p. 185). Recently the average scores on both have declined.

As a result of the disclosure of contents of the examinations now required by New York State's testing law, the Educational Testing Service no longer maintains the equating process. It has developed a process called "section preequating" to guarantee equivalence of scores by statistical formulation. Experimental sections of the Scholastic Aptitude Test, which will not count toward the student's score and will not be disclosed, will be equated with other parts of the same test and used in a new form the following year (Biemiller 1981c, p. 6).

Declining Scores
In considering possible causes for the extended decline in average test scores, the Advisory Panel on the Scholastic Aptitude Test Score Decline concluded that the test itself had not become inherently harder or less relevant to preceding training (Shane 1977). "The SAT score decline does not result from changes in the test or in the methods of scoring it" (Advisory Panel 1977, p. 8). The panel decided that shortening the test by one-half hour to include the separately scored Test of Standard Written English had not affected the scores. It reported technical analyses indicating an upward drift of eight to 12 points in scores so that the decline, as indicated by the scores, had probably been underestimated. The panel attributed the decline to a variety of factors, including less rigorous high school curricula, lower standards, inflated grades, less qualified teachers, and forces beyond the control of the schools (turbulent times, changes in family life, and vastly increased amounts of time spent watching television) (Advisory Panel 1977, pp. 44–48).

In their publications, testing organizations warn against using standardized test scores as a broad measure of the effectiveness of elementary and secondary education. Such tests, they remind us, are specifically designed to predict a student's likely performance, as indicated in academic grades, during the first year of college. Nevertheless, the high visibility of the Scholastic Aptitude Test in particular—along with its built-in comparability over several decades—makes it an important education indicator. The National Commission on Excellence in Education, for example, pointed to a virtually unbroken decline from 1962 to 1980 on the SATs, declines on College Board achievement tests in such subjects as physics and English, and a decline in the numbers and proportions of students demonstrating superior achievement on the SATs (*Chronicle* 1983f, p. 11). Similarly, other reports regarded falling test scores as a primary symptom of the nation's poor educational health (Farrell 1983f, 1983g; Task Force 1983).

The overall declines are unmistakable. From 1967 to 1982, the average SAT verbal score dropped 40 points, from 466 to 426, and the average SAT math score dropped 25 points, from 492 to 467. Looking at an earlier 15-year period, the advisory panel reported that, when standard deviation was taken into account, the decline meant that only one-third of the test takers in 1977 did as well as one-half the test takers in 1963 (1977, p. 5).

Nevertheless, it is important to break down recent results further to ascertain hidden trends or harbingers of change. The 1982 scores indicate a very slight improvement over the 1981 scores (SAT verbal scores up two points, SAT math scores up one point). The average total score on the Test of Standard Written English rose from 42.2 to 42.3 between 1981 and 1982, the first time since the test has been given. The average of scores on achievement tests also rose, up five points to 537, the highest since 1976 and 10 points above 1973 (College Board 1982c, p. 6). Although these point gains are small compared to the size of the declines, they are the first upward movement in nearly two decades. Officials of the College Board greeted them with "cautious optimism that the rise may presage the end of the long decline in scores" (Biemiller 1982c, p. 1).

Variations in Scores
The test performances of men and women vary. Of the 1 million students who took the SAT in 1982, 52 percent were women, a proportion that has steadily increased over the last decade. The larger number of women taking the

test may have affected average scores. In 1967, the average SAT verbal score for women exceeded that for men by five points (468 compared to 463); now the average for women falls behind the score for men by 10 points (421 compared to 431). From 1981 to 1982, however, the average SAT verbal score for women rose three points, compared to one point for men. On the SAT math portion, the average score for men rose one point from 1981 to 1982, but the score for women did not change. The gap between scores for men and women on the SAT math portion has also grown significantly, from 37 points in 1967 to 50 points in 1982. Among the students in the top tenth of their high school classes, the gap is even greater: The average math score for men exceeds that for women by 64 points (College Board 1982c, p. 5).

Concerns of Minorities
The performance of minority students on standardized aptitude and achievement tests continues to be an area of concern and controversy. The Advisory Panel on the Scholastic Aptitude Test Score Decline specifically examined allegations that the changing composition of the test-taking population had caused scores to drop. The national thrust to more universal access to higher education in the mid-1960s meant that a cumulatively larger proportion of students with relatively low grade point averages went on to college. In 1952, only one-half the school age population graduated from high school, and only one-quarter of those went on to college. In 1970, three-quarters graduated from high school, and one-half of those went on to college (Advisory Panel 1977, p. 13). Furthermore, less selective colleges were requiring students to take standardized tests for admission. Thus, test takers were no longer students heading only to the Ivy League but also to state universities and even open-admission community colleges.

The Advisory Panel concluded that the changing composition of the college-bound population had affected the average test scores but for a more limited time and to a lesser extent than assumed. The panel proposed a "two-decline" theory that was supported by similar patterns in the scores of other major standardized tests, notably those of the American College Testing Program.

- Between 1963 and 1970, the largest part (between two-thirds and three-quarters) of the SAT score decline was identified with compositional changes in the mix of the SAT test-taking group, both in terms of scoring groups and in plans for going to college.
- Between about 1972 and 1977, comparatively little (one-fifth to one-third) of the score decline could be attributed to the changing composition of the test-taking group (Advisory Panel 1977, p. 20).

In the latter period, declines were registered across the board, among high and low achievers, high and low incomes, blacks and whites, students in public, private, large, and small schools, in both academic and vocational courses.

Although the overall downward trend was linked to many educational and societal factors affecting both white and black students, the historical gap in test scores remained alarming. In view of the public interest in the issue, the College Board in 1982 for the first time released an analysis of the performance of racial and ethnic groups on the Scholastic Aptitude Test (Biemiller 1982d; College Board 1982c, pp. 7–8). Based on the class of 1981, 18.1 percent of which belonged to an ethnic minority, the results showed over a 100-point gap between the scores of whites and those of blacks. On the SAT verbal portion, whites averaged 442, blacks 332; on the SAT math portion, whites averaged 483, blacks 362.

But once again, the gross indicators must be considered in context. The College Board also issued for the first time information on the median income and median years of parental education of students taking the Scholastic Aptitude Test. The figures confirm the link, often cited by test opponents (Nairn 1980) between minority status, income, and test scores. (Release of this type of break-down had been resisted by test producers lest the statistics be misinterpreted or used to obscure the significant number of minority students who scored well.) For white students, parents' median income was $26,300, compared to $12,500 for blacks. Fathers and mothers of white students had completed 14.2 and 13.4 years of schooling, respectively, compared to 12.2 and 12.4 years completed by the fathers and mothers, respectively, of black students. Upon publi-

The performance of minority students on standardized . . . tests continues to an area of concern and controversy.

cation of the figures, George H. Hanford, president of the College Board, expressed hope "that the data, to the clear advantage of minority youth, will serve to illuminate the extent and nature of the educational deficit this nation must overcome" (Biemiller 1982d; Kurtz 1982a).

Shortly after issuing its analysis of minority performance, which was generally announced in articles emphasizing the 100-point gap between white and black students, the College Board released scores on the 1982 examination. They showed not only that the national averages were up for the first time in decades but also that much of the increase could be attributed to strong showings by minority students. Overall, the SAT verbal score rose two points, but verbal scores of black students rose nine points; the SAT math score rose one point, but math scores of black students rose four points. Between 1976 and 1982, the scores of white students declined (451 to 444 on SAT verbal, 493 to 483 on SAT math), while the scores of black students gained (332 to 341 on SAT verbal, 354 to 366 on SAT math), with much of the increase coming recently (Biemiller 1982e; Kurtz 1982b).

For many years, the disparity between white and black students' performance on standardized aptitude tests used for college admissions has been the object of analysis and action. Major criticisms have focused on a variety of issues:

- *Cultural bias:* Researchers have questioned the existence of a standardized test of vocabulary when there is no such thing as a standard vocabulary (Hilliard 1979, 1980, 1982).
- *Lack of participation by minorities:* The NAACP has called for a greater role for black psychometricians in the design and construction of standardized tests (1976, p. 20).
- *Effects of previous schooling:* Less progress has been made here. Minority students generally suffer from inadequate secondary school preparation. Fewer enroll in college preparatory courses. Court cases involving minimum competence tests have taken into account the effects of inadequate training on test performance.

Recent evidence seems to indicate some—albeit small—improvement in all these areas.

Changes

Organizations like the NAACP have recently developed a new approach to standardized testing that focuses on improving the performance of minority test takers rather than on changing the nature of the test. In 1983, the NAACP launched a program to provide inexpensive coaching for low-income students preparing to take either the SAT or ACT examinations. Designed by black psychometricians in cooperation with the Educational Testing Service, the project offers 14 three-hour coaching sessions; the fee for the course is applied to the cost of registering to take either test (Biemiller 1983b; NAACP 1983b). Project organizers also plan an evaluation to help determine what factors influence black students' performance. The beneficial effects of coaching are not clear (DerSimonian and Laird 1983; National Research Council 1982, pp. 196–98, 200), although some studies indicate that low students benefit most (NAACP 1983b, p. 5). It is known that a student can raise his score 15 to 30 points simply by retaking a test so that the experience gained in test-taking skills may prove useful. Additionally, because the costly coaching courses are usually the province of students from higher-income families, the NAACP program is another way to tackle the economic aspects of the gap in scores (Raspberry 1983a). It also involves parents. Parents are expected to participate in an orientation session and to agree that students will attend all the sessions and complete the assignments. The initial program is funded by a grant from the New York Community Trust. The NAACP hopes to attract additional financial support and to establish similar programs in areas with a large black population and an active NAACP branch.

The movement for testing legislation has also reflected a concern for the effects of testing on minority students. As early as 1974, the NAACP called for a moratorium on standardized testing until tests were corrected for cultural bias (NAACP 1976, pp. 2, 5; NAACP 1983a, p. 2). It also recommended that the testing industry take steps to improve its tests and the use of its tests by:

- providing specific data regarding predictive validity (do they predict accurately what they promise?), content, and prescriptive ability on various types of standardized tests
- providing separate validity coefficients for ethnic groups where standardized assessment results in the disproportionate sorting of groups according to ethnicity
- supporting an independent research and development corporation to identify problems of assessment affecting minority groups
- abiding by the principle of informed consent, by fully describing test objectives and procedures
- making clear in all descriptive information concerning a test the specific uses for which the test is designed, the specific limitations of the test instrument, and how test results should be interpreted
- adopting a fair testing code covering test construction, standardization, administration, use and interpretation, and research (NAACP 1983a, pp. 5–6, 25–28).

The concerns of the NAACP dovetailed with those of other powerful interests (Lerner 1980, pp. 121–23). The National Education Association opposed the use in public schools of standardized tests that were biased or used to compare schools and teachers, as the sole criterion for graduation or promotion, or as the basis for pay raises or promotions for teachers. It stated that historically tests have been used to differentiate rather than measure performance and have prevented equal educational opportunities for all students, particularly minorities, lower socio-economic groups, and women (NEA 1982, p. 51). As an alternative to standardized norm-referenced tests, it favors criterion-referenced tests carefully designed to test students' performance on developed curricula. It supports testing laws that include provisions for test takers to receive a copy of test questions, scores, and rationales for correct answers. Fred Hargadon, of the College Board, however, called the NEA's position "one more attempt to make it difficult for the public to render independent judgment on the efficacy of schools" (1981a, p. 102).

The attack by Ralph Nader's associates on standardized testing and on the Educational Testing Service in particular saw testing as a big business, students as unprotected consumers, minorities as disadvantaged victims, and the American public as unwitting dupes in a massive educational fraud (Fields and Jacobson 1980). The vehemence and comprehensiveness of the Nader group's report called public attention to the widespread use of tests in American life and the potential for the misuse of tests (Nader and Nairn 1980; Nairn et al. 1980). In particular, Nader's associates objected to equating test scores with intelligence and emphasized the correlation between a student's performance on a standardized test and his family's income level. The report has been criticized on many grounds (Lerner 1980), including its neglect of the distribution of students' scores at all income levels and its overestimation of their influence (Brandt 1980, p. 655).

The testing law passed by New York State anticipated some of Nader's concerns and recommendations. It requires that a test producer file the contents of a test with the state commissioner of education within 30 days of the test's administration and that questions and correct answers as well as the student's answers be disclosed to the student upon request. In the short run, test makers feared that disclosure would eliminate their ability to reuse test questions and would force a cutback in the number of test administrations. In fact, the number of administrations was cut back (Scully 1979a), and some testing companies were forced out of business in the state altogether (Fitzgibbon 1981). Minority students have not sought test information as much as hoped or expected, although the ease with which they may do so has been shown to significantly affect the number requesting it. Researchers have benefited from access to old tests in conducting research on the effects of coaching (Powell and Steelman 1983, p. 33).

The legislation has produced additional benefits. Although the Educational Testing Service opposed New York's law, it has been able to produce new tests and to restore the number of administrations of aptitude tests (Biemiller 1981c, p. 6). In April 1981, the College Board decided that students nationwide, not merely in regulated states, could request copies of their own and official answers on the Scholastic Aptitude Tests. This decision followed an earlier one to disclose answers to the Preliminary Scholastic Aptitude Tests (PSATs consist of questions from previous SATs) (Biemiller 1981b). In November 1981, Gregory R. Anrig, the president of the Educational Testing Service, proposed that testing organizations voluntarily prepare and abide by a code of fair testing to further the principle of openness in testing, seeing such a code as an alternative to federal regulation that might entail undesirable bureaucratic intrusion (Biemiller 1981e).

As part of its efforts at self-regulation, the Educational Testing Service invited a committee of outside educators to evaluate its compliance with its Standards for Quality and Fairness. Chaired by former Commissioner of Education Harold Howe II, the committee concluded that the ETS was doing a good job. It urged, however, greater efforts to inform the public about standardized tests and to discourage the misuse of tests, particularly by colleges that set an absolute cutoff score for admission (Biemiller 1982b).

For several sessions of Congress, Representative Ted Weiss (D.–N.Y.) has proposed a federal educational testing act, patterned after New York's law. The bill introduced in 1983 was identical to H.R. 1662 introduced in the 97th Congress in 1981. The testing agency would be required to submit information to the Secretary of Education and to provide information to each test taker, including:

- the purpose of the test
- the subject matter of the test and knowledge and skills being tested
- correlation of data on students' grades and test scores
- career performance and test scores, margin of error
- the ability of a test preparation course to improve students' scores
- how scores will be reported
- how background information on students will be reported
- students' rights of privacy
- how long students' scores will be kept
- time in which students will receive scores
- comparison of students' performance according to major income groups
- notice how a student may receive his own answers and the official answers, and how he may appeal or review his score.

The testing industry opposes such federal legislation, as does the Task Force on Ability Testing of the National Research Council (National Research Council 1982, p. 200).

Currently, handicapped students are raising issues about the validity and administration of tests comparable to those raised earlier by minority students. Similarly, the testing industry is responding with concerns about high costs and the lack of feasibility (*Higher Education Daily* 1982d; National Research Council 1982, p. 232).

Despite progress on several fronts, problems remain. The inordinate attention paid to the discovery of two errors on recent aptitude tests and the subsequent readjustment of scores obscure a more fundamental issue (*Chronicle* 1981b; Jacobson 1981b, p. 1). The question remains how standardized test scores are used and how they fit into the admissions process as a whole.

Standardized test scores are the most highly visible indicator of education. They assume extra importance because they are administered nationwide and at the key transition point between high school and college. Ironically, the demands for testing legislation by test opponents and opposition to such laws by the testing industry may have increased the public's perception that test scores dominate the college admissions process. The debate has obscured the degree to which test opponents and the testing industry agree on the use of test scores:

- that college admissions personnel *should not* rely too much on test scores in selecting students
- that college admissions personnel *should* consider a variety of objective and subjective factors in making decisions about admissions.

Recent reports demonstrate that generally (1) more institutions require students to take standardized tests than may be necessary, (2) even at selective institutions standardized test scores are only one criterion among many used in the admissions process, and (3) colleges need to articulate clearly their policy on admissions and how it fits with the institution's academic mission.

In recent years, the number and proportion of high school graduates going on to college has risen dramatically. So has the number of students taking standardized tests for college admissions. In 1978–79, almost 2 million SATs and ACTs were given (with an unknown number of students taking both). The American College Testing Program estimates that about 90 percent of the nation's 1,700 four-year undergraduate colleges require applicants to take either the SAT or the ACT (National Research Council 1982, p. 184). The national average of the scores of this large group stands in sharp contrast to the enormous diversity among the students themselves—in ability, in previous training, in educational and career goals (National Research Council 1982, p. 237). Over the last 20 years, as the college-going population has expanded and diversified so have the systems of education to which they apply. The number of possible combinations of students and colleges has therefore increased geometrically. The number of factors to be considered by both colleges and students has also increased. This chapter focuses on how institutional diversity and student diversity tend to undermine over-reliance on standardized test scores. And it considers possible new forces that will affect the admissions process.

Institutional Diversity
In contrast to the single, all-important test score portrayed by test opponents, representatives of the testing industry emphasize the autonomy and diversity of American institutions of higher education in their design of curricula, admissions policies, and standards for hiring faculty (Hargadon 1981a, p. 99). Practices followed in the admissions process are diverse in several ways:

- Institutions use different criteria in different combinations;
- Institutions use similar criteria but accord them different significance (Hargadon 1981a, p. 100).

Which criteria are applied and what weight they are given are affected by the type of institution and the number and quality of applicants.

A survey conducted in 1979 provided a comprehensive picture of admissions policies and practices nationwide (American Association/College Board 1980; *Chronicle* 1981a; Hargadon 1981b, pp. 1114–16). The 1,463 responding institutions reported admissions practices falling into three categories:

- *Open door:* All who wish to attend are admitted without review of conventional academic qualifications, or any high school graduate or equivalent is admitted (34 percent of respondents).
- *Selective:* A majority of applicants who meet some specific level of academic achievement or other qualification beyond high school graduation are admitted (56 percent).
- *Competitive:* Only a limited number of those applicants who meet specified levels of academic achievement or other qualifications beyond high school graduation are admitted (8 percent).

. . . more institutions require students to take standardized tests than may be necessary . . .

Institutions of different sorts fell at different points along this range of selectivity. While 34 percent of all responding schools were open door, 89 percent of the two-year public colleges fell into this category. Seventy percent of four-year public institutions had either an open door or selective admissions policy, whereas 90 percent of four-year private institutions had either a selective or competitive admissions policy. Only 56 percent of all institutions reported a selective policy, but at public and private four-year institutions these figures were 70 percent and 77 percent, respectively. These figures mean a huge area exists in which admissions personnel must consider and select among applicants who meet or exceed some level of academic qualification beyond high school. If test scores were the only factor considered, the job could be done by computer, saving endless hours of agonizing decisions (National Public Radio 1981) and substantial amounts of staff salaries. The question then is on what basis a particular institution will decide to admit a particular student. It is already known that a well-developed test may be a good predictor of performance of people in the aggregate but a poor predictor of the performance of any particular individual (National Research Council 1982, p. 237).

Colleges of all sorts compiled records, including the high school transcript, evidence of high school graduation or its equivalent, and standardized test scores. To a lesser degree, schools called for letters of recommendation, personal essays, autobiographies, or interviews. How this information was used and the minimum standards reported, however, varied with institutional needs and ambitions. The minimum academic standards differed between two-year and four-year colleges surveyed with lesser differences between public and private institutions in each sector. But schools reported less variation in *minimum* academic standards than might be supposed. Although many more four-year private institutions (58 percent) reported having a grade point average standard than did two-year public institutions (6 percent), the minimums themselves were very close: 2.0 and 1.9, respectively. Similarly, the average percentile requirement for high school class rank was 39 for two-year public colleges compared to 44 for four-year private ones. The largest variation appeared in minimum scores on standardized tests. At two-year public colleges, the reported minimums were 650 SAT combined score or 15.5 ACT composite score; at four-year public institutions, they were 740 SAT and 16.2 ACT; and at four-year private institutions, they were 754 SAT and 16.4 ACT (*Chronicle* 1981a).

The closeness of announced minimum standards means that admissions officers at institutions that are "competitive" or "selective" still retain a great deal of discretion in considering the various types of information provided by an applicant. The study made a start at compiling empirical evidence as to how institutions weigh and use test scores, high school records, and supplementary information (Hargadon 1981b, p. 1114). The three most significant considerations, according to the survey, were academic performance in high school, scores on aptitude tests, and the pattern of high school subjects.

- *Academic performance in high school* was considered the single most important factor or a very important factor in admissions decisions by 84 percent of four-year private institutions and 77 percent of four-year public institutions.
- *Scores on standardized aptitude tests* were considered the single most important factor or a very important factor by 55 percent of four-year private institutions and 63 percent of four-year public institutions.
- *The pattern of high school subjects* was considered the single most important factor or a very important factor by 38 percent of four-year private institutions and 25 percent of four-year public institutions.

The other characteristics and credentials mentioned, including interviews, essays, letters of recommendation, declared major, and ability to pay tuition and fees, were significant factors to varying degrees, but all fell far behind high school record, test scores, and high school program. To make the admissions brew even richer, each type of institution reported offering admission to less qualified applicants from specific groups, including athletes, relatives of alumni and faculty, racial or ethnic minorities, disadvantaged or physically handicapped persons, students with a particular talent, and older students.

Most colleges follow a three-part sorting process for

considering applicants. The Committee on Ability Testing described this breakdown as the presumptive-admit category (for students with strong academic credentials), the hold category (for students with less outstanding records but with special qualifications reported in supporting materials), and the presumptive-deny category (for students whose credentials appear weak) (National Research Council 1982, p. 185). Willingham and Breland dubbed these categories "likely," "uncertain," and "unlikely" (1982, p. 5). The University of Maryland has a group of preferred admits (applicants with high grade point averages and high SAT scores), regular admits (a space-available category for applicants who have lower scores and grades but an unusual talent, including athletic ability), and individual admits (a category for applicants who do not meet the university's regular standards but who may constitute up to 15 percent of the university's systemwide enrollment). "Threes" dominate the admissions process at Dartmouth College. Three yes votes by three admissions officers mean acceptance, three no votes rejection. At a round table where the bulk of applications are individually discussed, an applicant may be put in one of three drawers with increasing likelihood of acceptance (National Public Radio 1981).

In this plethora of criteria, standardized test scores are one among many and are not necessarily of primary importance. The assumption that test scores exert powerful influence over the lives of millions of people is false. Despite the vast changes in the number and kinds of students applying to college, ". . . almost all students who apply for admission to college are admitted to some institutions; the tests actually keep few if any applicants out of college altogether" (Harnett and Feldmesser 1980, p. 3). And, contrary to another stereotype, most students apply to only one or two institutions, and most institutions admit most of the students who apply to them. Fewer than 10 percent of four-year institutions admit fewer than half their applicants, while about one-third are virtually open door (Harnett and Feldmesser 1980). The do-or-die role of test scores described by test opponents appears to have a limited applicability.

Selectivity can take various forms. It can refer to the proportion of applicants chosen for admission or to the mean SAT scores of those students who enroll. And the two need not coincide. Studies show that even colleges generally regarded as the most selective have a fairly high acceptance rate. The selective institutions belonging to the Consortium on the Financing of Higher Education (including Stanford, Duke, MIT, and Williams), for example, report overall a high percentage of acceptances (69 percent of applicants admitted to at least one of the institutions in 1973–74). An institution may admit a large proportion of applicants but be "selective" as indicated by the academic ability of its student body. Examples include large institutions like the University of Chicago and small liberal arts colleges like Reed College whose entering students have higher mean SAT scores than those entering Stanford, which admits a smaller proportion of applicants (Harnett and Feldmesser 1980, p. 5). Further, the same institutions that are most selective in either sense tend to be those that emphasize the importance of flexible admissions criteria. Many of these institutions routinely reject candidates with high scores. For example, the 30 institutional members of the consortium reported turning down 430 applicants with SAT verbal scores between 750 and 800 while admitting in the same year 5,531 applicants with verbal scores between 500 and 550 (Brandt 1980, p. 657). In their analysis of the admissions decisions of nine selective colleges, however, Willingham and Breland found less reliance on nonquantifiable personal accomplishments than institutional policies suggested (1982).

Self-selection is an important aspect of the admissions process. At some institutions asking applicants to submit SAT or ACT scores, the test requirement may have more influence on whether a student applies than on whether the school is likely to admit him. Some observers regard this factor as a beneficial use of standardized test scores. Test scores may help students gain a more realistic idea about their potential for college success (Ebel 1982, p. 22) or may encourage students to raise their educational sights (Brandt 1980, p. 657) or may confirm what students already know. ". . . Many students make decisions about college long before they see SAT scores. It's not as if SAT scores come out of the dark, as if before the scores students don't know how they are doing relative to other students" (David Wise quoted in Paul 1983, p. 23). This view coincides with the fact that despite widespread grade inflation, the distribution of standardized test scores roughly follows class rank. Test scores correlate dramatically with subsequent dropping out. Scores are comparable between students who do not attend college and those who attend but drop out (Manski and Wise 1983). Sensitive and knowledgeable high school counseling is essential to prevent low-scoring students from deciding not to apply to college where nonquantifiable factors, such as character, creativity, persistence, or unusual talent, would make the student a likely candidate for admission nonetheless. That statement is true for students in general and for minority students in particular.

The clear thrust of recent reports and recommendations is that institutions across the range of selectivity should reconsider and clarify their use of standardized test scores in the admissions process. It is particularly hard to justify a required test score for admission to an open door institution. But such requirements exist, suggesting that schools may be using test scores for inappropriate purposes—to create an aura of selectivity for example—or for information that could better be obtained in other ways. Because it is known that a student's high school record is the best indicator of success in the first year of college, nonselective institutions can rely on the information about grade point average or class rank they would ordinarily obtain. Furthermore, standardized aptitude tests are not designed for diagnostic purposes so that questions about remedial work or class placement might better be answered by tests created for that purpose administered after the student has enrolled. Additionally, a requirement that an applicant take a standardized test for admission to an open door college falls most heavily on the very-low-income students best served by such an institution. Harnett and Feldmesser urged that more research be done on the actual and claimed uses of standardized tests because so many schools require them but so few rely on them (1980, p. 6). The Committee on Ability Testing of the National Research Council went a step further in its conclusions on admission to undergraduate institutions:

> *Despite the lack of selectivity in many colleges, the vast majority of them continue to require applicants to*

submit SAT or ACT scores. To the extent that scores are not used, students who are not planning to apply to selective schools are incurring unnecessary expense and inconvenience. There is also danger that students with poor or mediocre test scores may be discouraged from applying even to nonselective institutions in the mistaken belief that their chances of being admitted are small (National Research Council 1982, pp. 198–99).

The committee recommended that college admissions officers examine their policies on testing and determine the usefulness of requiring applicants to take admissions tests (Biemiller 1982a; National Research Council 1982, p. 201). At least one state has considered and rejected a proposal to reduce the number of students having to take standardized tests for admission to its public universities. The Iowa Board of Regents in 1981 voted down a plan whereby only students in the bottom half of their class would be required to take the SAT or ACT, although the state has to admit any graduate in the top half of his class regardless of test scores (Biemiller 1981a).

Student Diversity
Selective institutions have also been urged to reconsider their admissions policies. These colleges are expected to be most adversely affected by economic retrenchment and by projected declining enrollments. Fuller consideration of applicants' personal qualities, such as leadership and creativity, is more a goal than a reality in current practice among selective colleges (Jacobson 1982a; Willingham and Breland 1982). By measuring a residual selection rate (a school's actual selection rate for a particular type of student minus the selection rate expected on the basis of high school rank and test scores alone), Willingham and Breland found that:

- Personal qualities played a greater role in decisions about admissions at the more selective of the institutions studied;
- Minority group status had the largest residual effect in decisions;
- Institutional affiliation (as for children of alumni) also had a positive effect, although economic or social standing did not;

- Noteworthy extracurricular accomplishments during high school affected the selection of relatively few applicants (1982).

Distinguishing between applicants whose admission was initially judged likely/uncertain/unlikely, they found that background characteristics (alumni ties or minority status) resulted in preference for unlikely or uncertain admits. Personal achievements (such as demonstrated leadership qualities and outstanding references) more often determined choices between applicants with otherwise similar academic credentials.

Opponents of standardized admissions tests have rightly observed that such tests do not measure nonquantifiable traits like creativity, persistence, personality, or special talents. The testing industry has emphasized the limited information provided by test scores and their usefulness in predicting only first-year success in college. The Willingham and Breland study confirms the need to use both types of indicators in college admissions. A student's high school record remains the best predictor of early success in college; when coupled with test scores, the predictive value is enhanced. Persistence to the sophomore year, however, was found to be largely unrelated to any pre-admission measure, a finding confirmed by the ACT College Outcome Measures Project study (Forrest 1982, p. 25), while "personal achievements measures were neither a useful substitute for nor a supplement to rank and test scores in predicting grades" (Willingham and Breland 1982, p. 7).

Institutions of all sorts must be more explicit about what criteria they are using to make decisions about admissions. For selective institutions, doing so involves determining how much weight particular characteristics and types of achievements should have in the admissions process. This step is essential for internal operations, but it is also important for public understanding as well. The extent to which the role of standardized test scores is misunderstood reveals part of the problem.

When people stop thinking of tests as panaceas or using them as scapegoats, when they understand that testing is a useful, but limited, means of estimating one of the

*characteristics of interests in selecting or assessing
people, i.e., ability or talent, then a good part of the
conflict about testing will be alleviated* (National Research Council 1982, p. 208).

A close scrutiny of institutional interests and practice may
reveal that some test requirements are unnecessary—
indeed counterproductive.

Public information about the process is also essential.
Some have suggested that individual institutions adopt
policies comparable to the "truth-in-testing" disclosures
now made by the testing industry. Explicit statements
about admissions criteria in packets sent to potential
applicants may demystify the role of standardized test
scores (Dixon 1981, p. 70). It may also reduce some of the
tension involved in the admissions process (Sacks 1978,
p. 9). The Committee on Ability Testing recommended that
college admissions officers inform applicants how test
scores and other sources of information are used in making
decisions. Students should know if tests are optional to be
able to decide whether to take them (National Research
Council 1982, p. 201). Statements on the importance of
personal qualities and achievements may encourage a
student with somewhat lower scores to apply.

Every admissions officer can point to students who were
accepted despite poor quantitative indicators and who
succeeded academically nevertheless (Brandt 1980, p. 656;
Wickenden 1980). Both colleges and their potential students would benefit from further analysis of which factors
made the difference in the initial decision about admission
and in the student's college career. Higher education is at a
turning point:

> *Colleges thus appear to be entering an era in admissions
> characterized by a less exclusive emphasis on academic
> competence and a more balanced concern with aca-
> demic standards and the wide range of personal quali-
> ties relevant to recruitment as well as selection* (Wil-
> lingham and Breland 1982, p. 3).

What the Committee on Ability Testing observed concerning minority students is true for the admissions
process generally: that fine distinctions based on numerical

predictors is a misuse of tests (see also Lerner 1980); that decisions about admissions must be made case by case; that the goal should be a delicate balance between "selecting applicants who are likely to succeed in the program, . . . recognizing excellence, and . . . increasing the presence of identifiable underrepresented subpopulations" (National Research Council 1982, p. 196).

New Issues and Ideas Affecting Admissions

New issues in admissions will center around the positive aspects of institutional development and the negative factors associated with declining enrollments and shrinking funds. Neither the limits of the potential student population nor the ingenuity of educational policy makers has been reached. Responses to changing conditions may prove beneficial, and lessons learned from experience in increasing minority participation may prove generally applicable.

New participants in the admissions process

High school admissions counselors and college faculty are among those recently suggested as part of the admissions team. Menacker, for example, urging better cooperation between high schools and colleges, recommended consultations between the college admissions officer and the high school guidance counselor. Such consultation would combine, on a decision about a particular admission, detailed knowledge of the college's requirements and in-depth familiarity with a student's overall record (1975, p. 52). Ebel recommended that students themselves participate in the process, an interesting proposal that would require institutions to compile and make available important background information.

> *Instead of imposing a decision, the admissions officer may simply recommend it, leaving the applicant free to accept or reject the recommendation. Apprised of the information on which the recommendation was based and of the implications of that information on probable success in the program, most applicants are likely to concur. If they do not, they assume the burden of proving by their achievement that admission was warranted (1982, p. 23).*

Ebel argued that this method would recognize at the outset the student's own responsibility for his education and would reward effort as well as aptitude.

Faculty are also being involved in the admissions process (Perry 1982). Some institutions have tied increases in salary to student enrollments in an effort to mobilize faculty in recruiting. Where some departments or programs are struggling for survival or where faculty positions are jeopardized by declining enrollments, the use of faculty in recruitment may involve risks (undue pressure or unfair inducement to enroll, for example) as well as benefits. Thus, faculty participation should involve appropriate training and supervision. Some institutions have found faculty members ill suited to this work (Menacker 1975, p. 184). Institutions seeking to attract outstanding high school students are also using faculty and administrators in recruitment (Hook 1983b; Hymowitz 1983; Zigli 1983). A recent development is to grant scholarships on the basis of ability to academically talented applicants regardless of their financial need. Public institutions may waive tuition to attract able students (*Washington Post* 1983f). Outstanding scholars and deans are used to demonstrate the institution's excellence and its personal interest in the future student.

Admissions and institutional development
This new role for faculty and administrators in admissions is part of a larger trend to relate a school's admissions policy to its institutional mission. In the developmental model proposed by Willingham and Breland, the recruitment, selection, and retention of students are part of a single process that defines both the student body and the institution's character (1982, p. 184). This method requires more specificity than merely going after the "best" students. An institution must articulate its academic mission, define institutional programs that will advance that mission, and describe with some specificity what type of students might benefit from and contribute to such an endeavor. Willingham and Breland see the use of personal qualities as a basis for targeted recruiting, but the essential matter is the institution's awareness of its own goals. Institutions like the University of Maryland, which is working to join the ranks of the nation's top 10 public

universities, see the quality of their student bodies as a measure of academic excellence (Muscatine 1983). So far, however, Maryland is concentrating on quantifiable achievements with a new policy of waiving tuition for students with a combined SAT score of 1,000, a Test of Standard Written English score of 50, and a high school grade point average of 3.0 (*Washington Post* 1983f). Developing better programs and attracting better students become interrelated parts of the overall process of institutional development.

NEW MEASURES OF ACHIEVEMENT

Colleges are instituting stiffer course requirements for admission and are considering the use of standardized *achievement* test scores as new measures of precollegiate academic preparation. More explicit course requirements suggest a new element of rigidity, while the use of achievement scores suggests a somewhat more flexible alternative to the traditionally required aptitude tests. Yet the two measures have in common:

- the need for a clearer picture of what students have actually studied and learned in high school;
- the hope that such a change will force high schools to overhaul their curricula and offer more demanding subjects.

The rationale for both is clear—that past achievement is the best predictor of future performance.

Courses Required for Admission
The National Commission on Excellence in Education strongly advocated that colleges and universities raise their admissions standards just as it urged that school boards and state legislatures strengthen requirements for graduation from high school:

Four-year colleges and universities should raise their admissions requirements and advise all potential applicants of the standards for admission in terms of specific courses required, performance in these areas, and levels of achievement on standardized achievement tests in each of the five basics (English, mathematics, science, social studies, and computer science) and, where applicable, foreign languages (Chronicle 1983f, p. 14; National Commission 1983, p. 27).

In an appearance at the University of Maryland, Secretary of Education Terrel H. Bell urged that institution to stiffen its entrance requirements for undergraduates (Muscatine 1983). But as some observers have noted, the trend to higher entrance requirements, including those at the University of Maryland, preceded the commission's support of such a move (Scully 1983). As of spring 1982, 27 state universities had increased their admissions requirements or had them under review. In 13 states, they included course requirements (Thomson 1982).

In addition to requiring higher test scores and high school grades, colleges and universities are expanding the number and type of courses they expect prospective students to take in high school. Reasons for the change include the needs to limit enrollment, to raise the level of preparedness of incoming freshmen, to reduce the amount of remedial work necessary at the college level, and to encourage secondary schools to improve their college preparatory courses. It should be recalled, however, that rigidity does not guarantee quality. Both Menacker and the Committee on Ability Testing registered a caveat concerning course requirements, noting that the Eight-Year Study, conducted during the 1930s, demonstrated that the *quality* of performance in *any* high school subject was a better predictor of performance than the particular courses taken (Menacker 1975, pp. 70–71; National Research Council 1982, vol. 2, p. 186). Nevertheless, the trend to stiffer and more specific course requirements is clear.

Following the 1981 recommendations of the Advisory Commission on Articulation between Secondary Education and College, *Ohio State University* grants unconditional admission only to students completing a college preparatory curriculum that includes at least four units of English and three units each of mathematics, science, social science, and a foreign language *(Higher Education Daily* 1982a; Scully 1981b, p. 13; Southern Regional Education Board 1982a, p. 6).

In *California,* state colleges and universities are introducing new course requirements. In fall 1984, freshmen entering the California state university system will have to have taken four years of English and two of mathematics. At the University of California, incoming students will need 15 rather than 11 high school units in academic subjects, including English, mathematics, laboratory sciences, foreign languages, history, social sciences, and fine arts (Scully 1981b).

Similarly, state colleges and the state university in *Maryland* are stiffening their course requirements to include 12 college preparatory courses, including four in English, two in laboratory sciences, and three each in the social sciences and mathematics *(Chronicle* 1982b; Feinberg 1983a). The University of Maryland, which in the past did not specify any high school courses, will work with local school administrators to designate which courses meet university requirements. Said one member of the state Board of Regents, "We're trying to put pressure downward (on the high schools) so there will be a better educational system for all. This is a vehicle to get a quality student body" (Feinberg 1982c). It also set new standards requiring a high school average of C and a combined SAT score of 650 but retained its rule permitting that 15 percent of each freshman class be admitted without meeting minimum requirements. The Southern Regional Education Board, which recommended cooperative action to raise admissions requirements, noted:

> *In the general climate of competition for students it will be difficult to gain adherence to higher standards by voluntary action of individual colleges. Recent action in Maryland to raise admission requirements at each public institution simultaneously is an example of needed coordination to prevent the sacrifice of standards* (SREB Task Force 1981, p. 18).

As noted earlier, Maryland has also approved the waiver of tuition for students meeting certain academic requirements, not to exceed 1.5 percent of full-time enrollment (*Washington Post* 1983f).

In May 1983, the *Massachusetts* Board of Regents of Higher Education adopted new admission standards for four-year state colleges and universities, including a sliding scale for high school class rank and standardized test scores. It voted to require applicants in 1987 to have completed 16 college preparatory courses (*Chronicle* 1983h).

Several steps must be taken along with such changes to ensure effective and equitable implementation:

- adequate lead time so that students may complete the courses required
- adequate information so that all students will know what is required
- adequate counseling so that minority students will not be adversely affected by the new requirements
- cooperation between university officials and local

. . . colleges . . . are expanding the number and type of courses they expect . . . students to take in high school.

school personnel, preferably before the final adoption of new standards.

The trend toward stiffer admissions requirements also appears to be affecting the traditionally "open door" community colleges. Most two-year colleges are instituting more rigorous standards for obtaining associate degrees. But some are seeking to improve students' skills before enrollment. In *New Jersey,* Essex Community College and Passaic County Community College have established standards requiring demonstrated math and reading skills at about the 8th grade level. New Jersey requires all institutions of higher education to place students who do not achieve a minimum proficiency on basic skills tests in remedial courses until they can do college-level work. The New Jersey Council of Community Colleges has established a committee to recommend to the state board of higher education revisions in the state policy that now guarantees admission to a two-year college to all high school graduates (Watkins 1982a). New Jersey's response to the problem of poorly prepared students entering two-year colleges is indicative of the recently noted shift to state-level policy making for the locally oriented community college (Cohen and Lombardi 1979, p. 25; Watkins 1983d).

Reservations about raising admissions standards and particularly about making course requirements more rigid have been expressed by college admissions officers and minority group spokesmen. The combined pressures of falling enrollment and increasing minority participation suggest that flexible admissions policies might be preferable. A *flexible admissions policy:*

- seeks the best students available from the diverse constituencies served by the university
- requires reliable information about the applicant's high school and acknowledges wide variations among schools
- emphasizes the complete educational readiness of an applicant and allows the admission of the brightest minority, foreign, older, and late-blooming applicants, regardless of courses or rank and without relying on a "discretionary" category.

In contrast, an *inflexible admissions policy:*

- places an unnecessarily heavy emphasis on admission
- neglects or works against a student's total preparation if it favors (by standards for grade point average or course requirements) students who attend weak high schools or take less demanding courses (Jacobson 1982b; Sjogren 1982b).

It can be argued that the move to more flexible admissions standards, which benefits higher education generally, was fostered by the need to identify promising minority students whose academic potential was not apparent from traditional numerical indicators. As seen earlier, minority groups have worked to improve tests and are now working to upgrade the test-taking skills of minority students.

The decision in January 1983 by the National Collegiate Athletic Association (NCAA) to set minimum standards for first-year students participating in intercollegiate sports was a move in the opposite direction. Starting in August 1986, the rule, unless amended, will require entering students to have a 2.0 (C) grade point average in 11 academic high school courses, including three courses in English, two in mathematics, two in social science, and two in natural or physical science (Crowl 1983). In addition, a student would need a combined SAT score of 700 or a composite ACT score of 15. The head of the Educational Testing Service, Gregory R. Anrig, opposed the use of a fixed cutoff score. He noted the disproportionate effect of such a policy on black athletes and proposed consideration of alternate admissions standards (Vance 1983a). The rule was severely criticized by presidents of black colleges that historically have used flexible admissions standards in response to the needs of economically disadvantaged and poorly prepared black youth. The National Association for Equal Opportunity in Higher Education, a group representing 114 historically black colleges, called for a repeal of the new requirements. It proposed alternatives that would not exclude black athletes from competition and would ensure that they receive an adequate education as well (Farrell 1983c, 1983d).

The dangers of an inflexible standard, such as that proposed by the NCAA, must be weighed *in advance* as institutions consider changes in admissions policy. Surveying the new requirements adopted or considered by state universities, Scott Thomson of the National Association of Secondary School Principals suggested possible benefits: a salutary effect on students' attitudes toward serious study in high school, a more workmanlike atmosphere, pressure from parents for higher standards, more attention to precollegiate counseling (1982, pp. 7–8). Raising academic standards while maintaining flexibility in college admissions policies will be a major challenge of the 1980s.

Achievement Tests Reconsidered
Educators are now considering achievement test scores as an alternative to standardized aptitude test scores in evaluating a student's preparation for higher education. As discussed earlier, the admissions testing program of the College Board began with subject-oriented achievement tests. The more recently developed examinations of the American College Testing Program are organized around subject areas. At present, the College Board offers one-hour achievement tests in the following subjects: European history, American history, biology, chemistry, English composition, literature, beginning mathematics, advanced mathematics, physics, French, German, Hebrew, Latin, and Russian. Like SATs, these achievement tests are presented in a multiple-choice format.

Only a small percentage of colleges, usually the most selective ones, require that students take one or several achievement tests. Only 0.5 percent of all institutions and 7 percent of four-year private institutions consider achievement test scores a very important factor in decisions about admissions (*Chronicle* 1981a).

Presently only a small percentage, about 20 percent, of students taking the SAT also take one or more achievement tests. They tend to be abler students. According to the profile of college-bound seniors in 1982, only one student in four who took the SAT had scores at least as high as the SAT average of those who took achievement tests (College Board 1982c, p. 6). In terms of SAT scores, the most able students took the achievement tests in advanced mathematics, physics, chemistry, and Latin. The relative popularity of the tests varies. In 1982, for example, the number of students taking the German test declined 19 percent, while the number taking Latin increased 20 percent. The average score for all tests rose five points to 537, the highest since 1976. Overall, the number of students taking achievement tests has declined by one-third since 1973 so that the rising score may reflect the self-selected nature of the test population (College Board 1982c, p. 6).

Achievement test scores in the 750–800 range have dropped (Whitla 1982, pp. 20–25). Between 1976 and 1981, upper scores dropped precipitously in almost all subject areas with the exception of physics, which had experienced an earlier decline (p. 23). Despite this downward trend in achievement scores, they are useful as an indicator of college success. At Harvard University, scores on achievement tests have been a better predictor of grades than the Scholastic Aptitude Test and recently have surpassed secondary school grades as an indicator as well. "From a national standpoint . . . achievement measures are a very important commodity in the educational marketplace and it is worth taking a serious look at the results of these tests" (p. 20).

Christopher Jencks is another advocate of increased reliance on achievement test scores. He argues that the SAT does not measure aptitude but rather vocabulary, reading comprehension, and quantitative reasoning, all of which reflect both formal and informal educational experience. "College applicants have never had either equal opportunities or equal incentives to master anything. A 'pure' measure of aptitude for higher education is therefore unattainable" (Jencks and Crouse 1982, p. 26). The Committee on Ability Testing of the National Research Council agrees. "While a distinction is often made between tests of aptitude and tests of achievement, this report is not much concerned [with] this differentiation, because ability is always a combination of aptitude and achievement" (National Research Council 1982, p. 10). Achievement tests measure aptitude as well as does the SAT, predict college completion better than aptitude scores, and are equally as good at predicting economic success for adults (something the SAT does not claim to do). What SAT scores are meant to do—predict freshman year college grades—can be done as well by achievement test scores. They can be used interchangeably, as the SAT and ACT often are now (Jencks and Crouse 1982).

Additional reliance on achievement test scores might also affect secondary school preparation. Tests related to specific subjects might encourage students to take their course work more seriously and might encourage schools to offer more demanding courses. Although achievement tests are now the domain of academically able students, changes in curriculum to prepare students for them might benefit students generally (Jencks and Crouse 1982, p. 34).

Standardized tests of achievement . . . should be administered at major transition points from one level of schooling to another and particularly from high school to college or work. The purposes of these tests would be to: (a) certify the student's credentials; (b) identify the need for remedial intervention; (c) identify the opportunity for advanced or accelerated work. The tests should be administered as part of a nationwide (but not federal) system of state and localized standardized tests. This system should include other diagnostic procedures that assist teachers and students to evaluate student progress (Chronicle 1983f, p. 14; National Commission 1983, p. 28).

Ironically, testing legislation has threatened the availability of achievement tests. Under the Lavelle Act, the College Board was obliged to disclose the questions and answers for one edition of each achievement test every three years. In March 1983, the College Board announced that it would stop offering nine of 14 achievement tests previously given in New York State because of the prohibitive cost of preparing new tests to replace those disclosed (Biemiller 1983a). Faced with the prospect of New York residents' traveling to adjacent states to take the discontinued tests, the New York legislature revised the law. Editions of the less popular achievement tests must be disclosed only every eight years instead of every three years; editions of tests taken by more than 5,000 students yearly (American history, biology, chemistry, English composition, beginning mathematics) must be released every five years (*Chronicle* 1983j).

COMPETENCE IN COLLEGE

Not only are educators increasingly concerned that students enter college better prepared. They are also looking at ways to improve the academic performance of students enrolled in two-year and four-year institutions. As at the high school level, they must define what skills are most important, develop programs or courses to foster those skills, and evaluate students and programs to determine an institution's effectiveness. At the college level, however, it is even more crucial that these efforts be undertaken in the context of a clearly formulated institutional mission. The programs at schools as diverse as Miami-Dade Community College, Harvard University, and Alverno College illustrate the importance of tailoring curricula to the articulated needs of the institution and its student body. Several methods are used to increase and measure the competence of college students:

- raising standards in existing programs, particularly at two-year colleges
- changing course requirements for graduation at four-year colleges
- instituting a competence-based curriculum at both two- and four-year colleges
- defining achievement in terms of a value-added approach.

By each of these means, educators are seeking to regain a measure of academic excellence, to restore coherence and quality to their programs, and to meet the varied needs of their students.

Higher Standards for Existing Programs
No type of institution in American higher education has a more diverse student body than the two-year community college. Founded as a locally based steppingstone to a four-year baccalaureate program, community colleges now provide vocational and career training, continuing education, remedial courses, and noncredit activities. Among the most dramatic changes in the community college sector has been its growth. Between 1968 and 1978, the number of new institutions grew by 250, and the number of students more than doubled, to 4.2 million (Cohen and Lombardi

1979, p. 24). The other vast change has been in its student body; increasing numbers of minority students, women, lower-income students, and working adults are enrolled (Knoell 1982, p. 7). With these demographic shifts have come changes in course offerings—away from liberal arts curricula, credit for which can be transferred to a four-year institution, toward occupational programs (Kissler 1982, pp. 19–20). Of total full-time and part-time students enrolled for any reason in credit courses, "[fewer] than 5 percent each year in states with thriving community college systems transferred as juniors to colleges and universities" (Cohen and Lombardi 1979, p. 25). This great hodgepodge of students, differing in ability, preparation, interests, and aspirations, has forced a movement toward competence at two-year colleges similar to that in American high schools.

While most community colleges adhere to the open door admissions policy that has been their hallmark, many are demanding more evidence of achievement from students in their course work. This evidence may mean merely a change in the grading system. A stricter grading policy instituted at Passaic County Community College in 1976, for example, resulted in probation or suspension for one-third of its students. Students not only received Ds and Fs for the first time but were required to demonstrate proficiency in reading, writing, mathematics, and speech. Despite short-run difficulties, Passaic's president reported long-term benefits: more students enrolling, more passing professional examinations, and more going on to complete four-year degrees (Middleton 1981).

Because of the apparently declining basic skills of college students, more community colleges are requiring remediation before students enroll in transfer courses that demand certain levels of reading, writing, and math skills (Knoell 1982, p. 15). The program instituted in 1979 at Miami-Dade Community College involved remedial work, curricular changes, and stiffened academic requirements (McCabe 1982, pp. 3–4; Middleton 1981). All new students, including part-timers, are tested, and those falling below what are regarded as "reasonable expectations" in math, reading, or writing for the start of college work must take basic skills courses. After developmental work, students must take five general education courses from a core group in the humanities, social sciences, and natural sciences. Before proceeding beyond the core, students are tested to show that their reading and writing skills have improved.

Students' progress is assisted by courses on career choices, study skills, and time management. It is closely monitored, and course load is restricted according to performance. A student who has completed seven credits but has not achieved a C average (2.0) and has not passed half his courses must reduce his load. A full-time student not making adequate progress after 17 credits is limited to nine credits per term. An unsuccessful student at 30 credits is told that the institution can do no more for him. Over the program's first 2½ years, 10,000 students were suspended (McCabe 1982, p. 4).

The program embodies six basic steps that Miami-Dade's president believes are essential to strengthening academic standards while maintaining open access (McCabe 1981, p. 10; Schinoff and Kelly 1982, p. 71). Colleges should:

- increase their expectations of students
- become more directive in their program designs
- implement variable timetables for completion of programs
- provide more information to students
- set strict guidelines for suspension and dismissal of students who fail to meet the college's standard of progress
- commit themselves to adhering to their standards (McCabe 1981).

While most community colleges adhere to . . . open door admissions . . . many are demanding more evidence of achievement from students . . .

At Miami-Dade, every student receives a report every term based on information submitted by faculty members and processed by computer. Students' progress is measured according to institutional standards. Students in trouble are urged to see counselors or instructors. The cost per pupil is low, and the program has had significant results: over half the students whose progress is initially described as unsatisfactory pass courses by the end of the term.

Minimum competence testing and stiffer course requirements are an important trend in the transition between two-year and four-year colleges. Preliminary results of a study being conducted by the American Association of Community and Junior Colleges indicate the need to upgrade associate degree programs both in general education and in the development of basic skills. It recommends that two-year colleges establish standards of competence and require students to pass tests to meet the standards before receiving their degrees (Watkins 1983c). Starting in August 1984, the Florida Department of Education will administer a basic skills test for students seeking either an associate degree or admission to the upper division of a state four-year institution. Requested by the state legislature and developed by faculty members of two-year and four-year institutions, the test will cover communications, computation, and reasoning. Since July 1983, California's community college system requires students to complete 18 rather than 15 units of general education courses, including writing and analytical thinking, to earn an associate degree. Students also have to meet standards for proficiency in reading, writing, and mathematics established by each college to graduate. A failing F grade has also been reinstated (Watkins 1982a).

Although the trend is to require all students in community colleges to meet higher standards, the programmatic gap between liberal arts and vocational students remains a problem (London 1978, 1982). Students in vocational courses need to be aware of the requirements and opportunities involved in taking liberal arts courses. "The goal is not to force students into transfer programs, but to advise them about educational and career opportunities at the baccalaureate level, including student aid, in relation to their own interests and ability" (Knoell 1982, p. 13). Community colleges therefore need to identify the particular needs of transfer students in the liberal arts and to reexamine their liberal arts courses for ways to make them more relevant and important to vocational students (Middleton 1979).

A report by the Southern Regional Education Board considered ways to facilitate *lateral mobility* for community college students between different types of programs at the same level. While the SREB was particularly concerned with the movement of minority students, the ideas presented would benefit all students:

- minimize a loss of credit in changing programs
- involve college personnel and community representatives in the development of policy

- include as many general education courses as possible in vocational and technical curricula
- emphasize competencies rather than normative grading
- require students to periodically reexamine their educational goals
- formulate and publicize relationships with other institutions on the transfer of credits and articulation of courses (Southern Regional Education Board 1977, pp. 12–13).

The SREB considered a broad commitment to students' mobility and a strong program of faculty and staff development essential to designing effective courses and procedures.

Even though transfer to the upper division occupies a less important place in the mission of the community college, *vertical mobility* can also be facilitated. This movement is particularly important for minority students, over half of whom enter higher education by way of a community college, and for students in states like Florida and California with elaborate community college systems. The transfer process has become more complex (Knoell 1982, p. 3). The transfer student faces increasingly stringent requirements for graduation from four-year institutions and stiffer competition from "native" students in high-demand majors. At Miami-Dade, the Advisement and Graduation Information System each term provides every student with a printout showing how he stands against Miami-Dade's graduation requirements, which are locked in at the time of his entry. It also compares the student's record with admissions requirements in a specified major at the 13 Florida universities to which Miami-Dade students usually transfer. By the terms of a statewide articulation agreement between the university and community college systems, the general education requirement of the baccalaureate degree is the responsibility of the community college awarding the associate in arts degree. A student entering an upper division program may not be required to fulfill additional general education courses but must comply with the requirements for the major field established by the university. This type of generally accepted lower-level transfer course may be preferable to specific articulation agreements between institutions (Knoell 1982, pp. 15–16). To ease the transition, Miami-Dade students earning an associate degree must now take a cluster of courses, similar to a major, totaling 24 credits of more demanding second-level work (McCabe 1982, p. 5; Schinoff and Kelly 1982).

Stiffer Course Requirements for Graduation

At four-year colleges, the trend is similar to the one in American high schools and in community colleges. Institutions are seeking to bring order to general education, described as a "disaster area" (Scully 1981a). Colleges are pulling back from the enormous latitude in course selection granted to students in the 1970s. But in reinstituting more sharply defined requirements, particularly for general education courses, each college needs to consider its own academic mission, the special needs of its students, and how policies can best advance the interests of each. Every institution must establish its own balance between commonality and diversity.

The circle of educational change is now closing. In the 1970s, the proportion of prescribed general education courses decreased, partly in response to students' demands for greater freedom. While requirements for major courses stayed fairly constant, general education requirements yielded to a growing component of electives. The job market also dictated that undergraduates prepare for a career. Students took electives related to their majors to prepare for admittance to graduate or professional school or to better their chances for employment. Fewer students studied literature, foreign languages, mathematics, and social sciences. They enrolled instead in such professionally oriented fields as business administration and computer sciences (Astin 1982a; Southern Regional Education Board 1979, p. 3). A similar pattern prevailed in the intentions of college-bound seniors in 1982 (College Board 1982c, p. 9). High school curricula followed the same trend, reducing general education requirements and increasing electives. For those and many other reasons (Advisory Panel 1977), freshmen were poorly prepared to handle college-level work. The coincidence of inadequate preparation and incoherent curricular standards prompted a reconsideration of what constitutes the basic academic program of a college and the basic academic accomplishments of its students.

The reexamination of general education today seems to stem more from a realization that undergraduate general education has become too unstructured, is dealing with students unprepared in the basic skills, and is lacking in central purpose than because of a fundamental rediscovery of the values of teaching the cultural heritage (Southern Regional Education Board 1979, p. 1).*

The core curriculum adopted by Harvard College in 1978 and implemented over four years provides an example of the process of adjusting requirements and of many possible configurations (Change Magazine Editors 1979). The quest for a core curriculum was based on Harvard's conception of an educated person, whose major attributes, described by Dean Henry Rosovsky, include the ability to think and write clearly and effectively, knowledge of some field in depth, critical appreciation of the ways we gain and apply knowledge about society, the ability to understand and think about moral and ethical problems, and awareness of other cultures and times. Students are expected to concentrate a substantial part of their work in a single subject as well as to take courses designated part of the core curriculum in five areas: literature and the arts, history, social analysis and moral reasoning, science, and foreign cultures. The 10 course requirements, with some overlap, are meant to constitute the equivalent of one academic year. "These different areas of the core curriculum are linked by a common question: How do we gain and apply knowledge and understanding of the universe, of society, and of ourselves? The underlying purpose of the core is to set a minimum standard of intellectual breadth for our students" (Change Magazine Editors 1979, p. 9). Students are also expected to demonstrate competence in expository writing and the application of mathematics and quantitative reasoning, and to acquire an elementary knowledge of computer programming.

*While changes are well underway at colleges of all sorts, a review of Brown University's 14-year-old "new curriculum," which allows considerable flexibility and continues to attract large numbers of applicants, is expected to produce few major changes (see Desruisseaux 1983b).

Nationwide, changes in course requirements outside a student's major reflect movement in two directions: away from narrow specialization and professional education toward broader educational purposes (Klein and Gaff 1982, p. 5) but also away from overbroad, unfettered discretion among limitless course offerings. Thus, the new requirements are simultaneously intended to be more broad and more narrow. In a survey of 2,102 colleges of all types, Klein and Gaff identified aspects of what they regarded as a "national revival of general education" (*Chronicle* 1982c; Magarrell 1982). These curricular changes involved:

- a larger portion of required general education courses or in some cases changed offerings within the same time frame
- additional structure and fewer choices for students, with most programs combining limited distribution, an interdisciplinary core, and required courses
- more liberal arts subjects, including increased requirements in the humanities, arts, natural sciences, and social sciences
- more attention to basic skills, including writing and mathematics, and advanced skills like critical thinking, problem solving, research/library skills, foreign language, computer literacy, and interpersonal relations
- qualitative changes toward more interdisciplinary approaches, global perspectives, nonlecture pedagogy, with general education courses taken over four years rather than confined to the first two years (Klein and Gaff 1982, pp. 4–7; Southern Regional Education Board 1979, p. 5).

A core curriculum or more sharply defined programs of general education thus suggest both a restoration of a shared educational experience (Boyer and Kaplan 1977) and a return to individual achievement of academic excellence. Klein and Gaff found a major interest in analytical thinking, including the ability to examine arguments and reason logically and critically, as well as in synthetic thinking, that is, the ability to make connections. They also found consideration of moral, empirical, and aesthetic modes of thinking. They contrast this return to rationality with the "relevance" and "narcissism" of earlier reforms (1982, p. 6). It should be observed as well, however, that the current movement also emphasizes originality and creativity rather than a rote mastery of predetermined solutions.

Critics of the trend toward a core curriculum or enhanced general education regard them as a step backward for education and bemoan their obeisance to the departmental structure and their failure to incorporate the insights derived from the experience of the last two decades. Reviewing proposals for restructuring curricula at 25 institutions, Barry O'Connell concludes:

> *Little institutional self-examination occurs, and when it does it covers a narrow range: what new courses are needed, what means can be devised to improve teaching, how best to cope with financial stringencies. Only a few documents inquire about the reasons for poor teaching, the fragmentation of the faculty, or the existence of thoughtlessly designed departmental majors. . . . The crucial questions—about the role of the university in maintaining inequality and about the desired ends of an undergraduate education—are left untouched* (Change Magazine Editors 1979, pp. 27–28).

Leon Botstein, president of Bard College and himself a proponent of greatly strengthened basic language training in college curricula (Watkins 1981a), has urged that the general education movement begin the task of "creative adaption of past models of curriculum and standards of education." Doing so would include incorporating the technological and scientific revolution into the liberal arts curricula, fighting inappropriate fragmentation of the curriculum by disciplines, and adding an aesthetic dimension to general education (Botstein 1982). In proposing alternative models for undergraduate education, Hall and Kevles state that a college curriculum must recognize the diverse interests of its heterogeneous clientele and include societal imperatives (1982, p. 37). Other observers emphasize the need to devise a future-oriented curriculum (Shane 1981).

Competence-based Curriculum

In contrast to the detailed course of distribution requirements being reinstituted in general education programs, some colleges are moving to a competence-based curriculum in the liberal arts (Knott 1975). Some disciplines, notably English, have developed a competence-based curriculum (Cooper 1981; Hibbs 1980). Alverno College, a small women's college outside Milwaukee, has put itself on the higher education map by devising a four-year degree program shaped around competencies rather than traditional disciplines (Loacker 1981; Olive 1978; Scully 1975). Each of these efforts involves a fundamental decision by school or department to determine what is basic, how it is to be taught or developed, and how mastery is to be measured.

Returning to higher standards need not be dull nor need it mean a return to old subjects or methods (Advisory Panel 1977, pp. 41, 46; Desruisseaux 1983a). Indeed, both proponents and critics of the current changes in program suggest that institutions should be more consciously imaginative about what they want to do and how they plan to go about it. Cross-disciplinary links need to be strengthened. Efforts to improve writing skills, for example, may involve a number of academic departments, requiring a new flexibility, not an old rigidity (Southern Regional Education Board 1982b; Whitla 1982, p. 6). Returning to quality and coherence may require blending old skills with new areas of study or fitting new technology to old disciplines. The possibilities are endless, united by more rigorous standards for skill and mastery of content.

The Value-added Approach

Although the general trend is to reinstitute more rigorous course requirements or to adopt a core curriculum, in most colleges traditional grading practices are still being followed. Traditional grading can be improved (Milton and Edgerly 1977), but some researchers are recommending and some institutions are using new methods of measuring and enhancing students' achievement. The most widely discussed is the value-added approach.

In contrast to letter or numerical grades that provide a static indicator of performance, the value-added approach measures changes in a student's performance from the beginning to the end of an educational experience (Commission 1982, pp. 24–25). Proponents argue that the value-added approach can be used at any academic level in conjunction with rather than instead of traditional grades. It can involve many sorts of assessment instruments, including objective or essay tests, oral examinations, or other indicators appropriate to the course of the program. In its simplest form, the value-added approach can involve an initial "pretest" to indicate the student's entering level of competence. This information would be used both for counseling and course placement and for later evaluation of a pupil's progress when compared with the student's "posttest" performance.

Unlike traditional course grades, which do not necessarily reflect what students have learned but merely rank them in relation to each other at a single point in time, before-and-after testing indicates whether and to what extent students are actually benefiting from their educational experience (Astin 1982b, pp. 15–16).

The value-added approach can benefit both students and schools. For students, the approach means that:

- Opportunities are not denied because of performance below the norm; a student's progress is gauged according to his own baseline; students at any level can show progress;
- A dynamic indicator of achievement is used in contrast to the static measure of standardized or exit tests;
- Feedback on the individual's performance can be used to foster additional improvements.

For institutions, the approach means that:

- Excellence is not restricted only to institutions with resources, prestige, or high-ability students (Astin 1982b);
- Detailed information about pupils' progress can help in program modifications;
- Methods of assessment can be diverse and flexible.

The value-added approach can be used on a short-term basis, as for a single course, or for a four-year academic career. It can be used by open admissions institutions or highly competitive ones.

Harvard University has applied the value-added concept. Supported by the Fund for the Improvement of Postsecondary Education, the Harvard project measured change between freshman and senior year on eight objectives of liberal education (which coincide to some degree with the aims of the core curriculum): (1) the ability to communicate with clarity and style; (2) the capacity to analyze problems by collecting relevant data and marshaling pertinent arguments; (3) a sensitivity to ethical considerations and the capacity to make discriminating moral and value choices; (4) an ability to master new concepts and materials across major disciplines; (5) a critical appreciation for the ways we gain an understanding of the universe, society, and ourselves; (6) a sensitivity to interpersonal relations; (7) the extent to which life experiences are viewed in a wide context; and (8) a broadening of intellectual and aesthetic interests (Whitla 1982, pp. 4–5).

Each of these areas required its own type of measurement, far surpassing in sophistication the type of pretest/posttest analysis that might be used for a single course. The results were extraordinarily rich, showing differences between majors, between men and women, between those who had taken a particular course and those who had not. Dividing students into three groups according to SAT/ACT scores, the project found significant gains by each, with the lowest group gaining most in fundamental writing and the ability to think effectively, the highest third gaining most in analytical ability, and the middle third falling between (Whitla 1982, p. 12).

The value-added approach is also useful at various types of institutions. Of the schools compared, students at Boston State College registered the strongest gains in performance between the freshman and senior years. Boston State's freshmen performed very poorly compared to the rest of the sample but ended in a strong and competitive position, confirming Astin's observation that the value-added concept enables us to identify excellence in a variety of settings.

The Harvard project links the value-added concept and

the goals of the core curriculum. Similarly, the College Outcome Measures Project of the American College Testing Program links students' competence and persistence to programs of general education (Forrest 1982). Organized in 1976, COMP aids colleges in improving general education, providing instruments to measure skills and knowledge, and offering support services. Two outcomes are expected from general education programs:

- Students should acquire the basic abilities and motivation needed to successfully complete courses in a chosen field of concentration and other requirements for graduation;
- Students should acquire the basic abilities and motivation needed to function effectively in a number of adult roles after graduation (Forrest 1982, p. 10).

COMP assessment instruments measure learning in six general areas: communicating, solving problems, clarifying values, functioning within social institutions, using science and technology, and using the arts. Colleges use COMP to evaluate the effectiveness of their general education programs, which can be done by testing a group of freshmen and retesting the group before graduation or by testing matched groups of freshmen and seniors.

In a study of 44 institutions of various types that had used COMP, analysts found a wide range of gains in average scores and varying rates of persistence. The results showed a correlation between high score gains and high persistence to graduation but a weak relationship between high score gains and persistence to sophomore year (Forrest 1982, pp. 24–25). Further, the results associated higher average score gains with institutions that:

- provide the most comprehensive program for orientation and advising
- devise student-oriented goals and proficiency exams
- require a large general education component and an even distribution of required courses
- offer formal remedial and off-campus instruction.

The report urged that institutions with general education programs state their expectations clearly in terms of benefits to students and analyze the results closely to see whether those objectives are being met.

COMPETENT TEACHERS

The national debate over teacher training and certification involves each of the issues already seen in earlier discussions of standards and course work at the high school and college levels: What skills and academic training should teachers have? How should they be measured? What is the appropriate role of standardized testing? What are the particular issues for minority students preparing to enter the teaching profession?

The problem of teacher training is multifaceted. Some aspects are similar to those of other professions. Questions as to what makes a good teacher, like those about what makes a good doctor, suggest that tangible measures of collegiate course work and standardized test scores do not tell much about intangible qualities of character, patience, perseverance, or creativity, which are also desirable professional traits. Unlike law or medicine, however, teaching is neither a high-prestige nor a high-salary profession. While entry to law school or medical school has become highly competitive (Sacks et al. 1978), interest in teaching has declined. Observers greet this decline with some ambivalence, attributing at least part of it to increased opportunities for women and minorities in fields that previously excluded them. Once there was a surplus of teachers; now a serious national shortage is predicted by 1985 (Watkins 1981b). Most teachers colleges have become general state colleges or state universities with the consequent loss of focus and identity for teacher training (Astin 1982b, pp. 24–26). The best students no longer choose to be teachers; of those who study education, the least able are more likely to complete the course (*Chronicle* 1983f, p. 14; National Commission 1983, p. 22).

Every major report reviewing the current state of high school preparation for college considers better teacher training essential to long-range improvements. The National Commission on Excellence in Education cited both the declining quality of America's teaching profession and the worsening working conditions of America's teachers. It recommended improved pay, career ladders, a better work environment, and incentives to draw and keep the most qualified people in the nation's schools. But it also recommended higher standards of performance for teachers:

Persons preparing to teach should be required to meet high educational standards, to demonstrate an aptitude for teaching, and to demonstrate competence in an academic discipline. Colleges and universities offering teacher preparation programs should be judged by how well their graduates meet these criteria (*Chronicle* 1983f, p. 14; National Commission 1983, p. 30).

It also recommended that decisions about salary, promotion, retention, and tenure be based on evaluation, including peer review, "so that superior teachers can be rewarded, average ones encouraged, and poor ones either improved or terminated" (*Chronicle* 1983f, pp. 14–15; National Commission 1983, p. 30). One recommendation is the designation of master teachers and their involvement in the preparation and supervision of teachers (*Chronicle* 1983g; Farrell 1983f). The concept of master teacher, including merit pay, has been strongly endorsed by President Reagan and is being pushed by Governor Lamar Alexander in Tennessee, where it is opposed by the affiliate of the National Education Association (Hoffman 1983; Shields 1983).

Unlike law or medicine, . . . teaching is neither a high-prestige nor a high-salary profession.

Better teachers must themselves be better trained, which means higher levels of academic accomplishment in addition to the traditional courses in educational theory and technique. All the academic areas in which students' preparation must be improved, including science, mathematics, and foreign languages, require many more teachers with specialization in the subjects (Rutherford 1983). A 1981 survey of 45 states found shortages of math teachers in 43 states, and half the newly employed math, science, and English teachers are not qualified to teach those subjects (*Chronicle* 1983f, p. 14; National Commission 1983, p. 23). Of 19 fields of study analyzed by the American College Testing Service, education majors ranked 14th in English ability and 17th in math ability (Raspberry 1983c).

The content and requirements of programs for education majors must be reconsidered. The Southern Regional Education Board recommended both an upgraded subject component for education majors and a reduced requirement for education courses for subject specialists seeking certification to teach. It urged:

- better cooperation between faculty in teacher education programs and faculty in arts and sciences departments who teach general education courses to future teachers during their first two years;
- streamlined certification regulations, including provisional certification for faculty in arts and sciences departments who teach general education courses to future teachers during their first two years;
- streamlined certification regulations, including provisional certification for arts and sciences graduates to teach in their major field in secondary schools while their performance is monitored or they take required professional courses;
- more flexible certification standards with increasing levels of subject competence in math and science for more advanced high school courses (SREB Task Force 1981, pp. 8–10; see also Winn 1983).

The National Commission on Excellence in Education recommended that recent graduates with degrees in math and science, graduate students, and industrial and retired scientists be used immediately, with appropriate preparation, to alleviate the shortage of math and science teachers (*Chronicle* 1983f, p. 15; National Commission 1983, p. 31). Virginia has already adopted a flexible teacher certification plan. Liberal arts graduates may be provisionally certified for two years to teach in secondary schools while they take nine semester hours in teaching methods and are observed and counseled by experienced teachers (Ingalls 1982).

The level of teachers' competence demonstrated by standardized test scores is a matter of continuing debate and concern (Boardman and Butler 1981; Witty 1982). As with all nationally normed tests, those used to certify teachers either for employment or promotion are subject to misuse, have a disproportionately adverse effect on minorities, and do not indicate nonquantifiable traits desirable in a professional teacher. Several years before the Supreme Court ruling in *Washington* v. *Davis* that employment tests must be job related,* a circuit court of appeals declared it unconstitutional for a school board to use Graduate Record Examination scores in hiring or

Washington v. *Davis*, 426 U.S. 229 (1976).

retaining teachers.* The court concluded that the GRE was neither a reliable nor a valid measure for choosing good teachers and had no reasonable function in the process of selecting teachers.

The more commonly used National Teacher Examination is specifically designed to measure the academic preparation of teachers. It too, however, may be misused. In a 1976 case,† the federal government challenged North Carolina's use of a cutoff score of 950 on the National Teacher Examination to determine the salary, retention, and tenure of teachers with substantial inservice experience and to determine the certification of prospective teachers with no experience (Manning 1977). Minority teachers and students fell below the cutoff in disproportionate numbers. In a friend of the court brief (Willens 1975), the Educational Testing Service, which prepared the test, defended the merits of the examination but opposed the use of a fixed cutoff score. According to the ETS brief, the National Teacher Examination as then constituted was prepared for prospective teachers with no professional experience. The brief detailed the steps taken by ETS to ensure against inherent racial or cultural bias (pp. 17, 29) and to include positive references to areas identified with minority groups (p. 17). As a subject-oriented test, the teacher examination was as much an indicator of the quality of teacher training programs as it was of the achievement levels of their graduates. The brief concluded:

> *If the educational institutions that the examinees attend do not impart the knowledge, or enough of the knowledge, required to answer correctly the questions on the National Teacher Examinations, then a low score will result, regardless of the race of the examinee* (p. 30).

The Educational Testing Service urged, as it does with its other standardized instruments, that a cutoff score not be used unless it could be validated against other criteria. It suggested that school district personnel weigh all evidence of a teacher's ability, including college record, recommendations, interviews, and student teaching experience, as well as test scores. The federal district court held that the

*Armstead v. Starkville Municipal Separate School District, 461 F. 2d 276 (5th Cir. 1972).

†U.S. v. State of North Carolina, 400 F. Supp. 343 (E.D. N.C. 1975), vacated, 425 F. Supp. 789 (E.D. N.C. 1977).

state of North Carolina had the right to adopt academic requirements and written achievement tests designed and validated to disclose the minimum amount of knowledge necessary to teach effectively. It concluded that the National Teacher Examination probably measured a critical amount of knowledge in an academic subject area and that a cutoff score could be established for the requisite knowledge. The Supreme Court's decision in *Washington* v. *Davis,* requiring that an employment test be demonstrably job related, caused this ruling to be vacated.

In a similar suit in South Carolina, the United States Department of Justice, acting on a complaint from the Equal Employment Opportunity Commission, along with the National and South Carolina Education Associations, sought to bar the use of the National Teacher Examination as a requirement for certification to teach grades K through 12. When suit was filed, a combined score of 975 was required to pass, with a score no less than 450 on either the common examination of basic academic knowledge or the subject area test. In 1976, the test was upgraded and higher scores were required, depending on the subject area, ranging from the 15th and the 30th percentile. Plaintiffs argued that the test discriminated against new black teachers. Overall, 60 percent of graduating seniors who took the test, but only 3 percent of the seniors graduating from the state's black colleges, passed in South Carolina. In April 1976, a three-judge panel ruled that the test was not discriminatory in intent although blacks failed to do as well as whites (King 1977). The case was appealed to the Supreme Court, which upheld the use of the National Teacher Examination in decisions about employment and salaries of teachers (McDaniel 1977; Witty 1982, p. 11).

Since a two-year study by the National Teacher Examination Policy Council appointed by the Educational Testing Service in 1979, the National Teacher Examination has been significantly changed. Since December 1982, the test has been made up of three parts instead of two:

- *Professional education* emphasizes the teacher as problem solver;
- *General education* tests math, science, social studies, literature, and fine arts, focusing on concepts rather than simple skills;

- *Communication skills* includes a multiple-choice English test, an essay, and listening and reading skills (*Phi Delta Kappan* 1981).

The test measures performance at an 8th or 9th grade level and is considered so elementary that some states, like Florida, have raised the minimum score required to pass (Harris 1983b). Administration of the test has been made more flexible. The three sections may be taken separately or together and as early as the sophomore year to allow students to improve their skills or change to another field (Witty 1982, p. 12).

According to the American Association of Colleges for Teacher Education, more than half the states have taken some action involving the use of standardized tests at some or all the key transition points for future teachers: admittance to a teacher education program, graduation from such a program, or initial teacher certification (Watkins 1983b). Most states in the South already use the test for hiring and certification. By 1985, 25 states are expected to have a similar teaching license examination.

Nationwide, minority students register significantly lower scores than whites. In California, the minority failure rate was 70 percent; in Arizona, 75 percent of blacks and native Americans failed, compared to 66 percent of Hispanics and 25 percent of whites. In Florida, only one-third of black applicants passed, compared to 90 percent of whites (Harris 1983b). In that state, a minimum competence requirement for a high school diploma has been upheld in court despite the disproportionately high failure rate of black students. Some critics have argued that the questions or problems on problem solving are culturally biased in favor of white middle-class values. Other suggest that the test reflects the culture in which minority teachers will have to function.

Standardized tests cannot measure patience, love of children and of learning, the ability to maintain order and a hundred other things that make up teacher competency. But the tests can measure whether a teacher has learned the basics of pedagogic technique (which we consider important, else why would we mandate education courses for teachers?) and whether a teacher has a solid grasp of the material to be taught (Raspberry 1983b).

Black educators and civil rights leaders caution against overreliance on tests and urge that further research is necessary (Boardman and Butler 1981, p. 67; *Higher Education Daily* 1982e; Witty 1982, pp. 19–23), particularly to determine the relationship between test scores of teacher college graduates and their later effectiveness as teachers.

As with the issue of teachers' preparation and performance on standardized tests, the question of competence has come full circle. Students in all grades need adequately trained teachers to maximize their academic potential. Teachers themselves need more rigorous preparation to develop the professional skills and mastery of subjects necessary to do their part in returning American education at all levels to its fundamental excellence and coherence.

BIBLIOGRAPHY

The ERIC Clearinghouse on Higher Education abstracts and indexes the current literature on higher education for the National Institute of Education's monthly bibliographic journal *Resources in Education*. Most of these publications are available through the ERIC Document Reproduction Service (EDRS). For publications cited in this bibliography that are available from EDRS, ordering number and price are included. Readers who wish to order a publication should write to the ERIC Document Reproduction Service, P.O. Box 190, Arlington, Virginia 22210. When ordering, please specify the document number. Documents are available as noted in microfiche (MF) and paper copy (PC). Since prices are subject to change it is advisable to check the latest issue of *Resources in Education* for current cost based on the number of pages in the publication.

Advisory Panel on the Scholastic Aptitude Test Score Decline. 1977. *On Further Examination*. New York: College Entrance Examination Board. ED 148 834. 837 pp. MF–$2.31; PC not available EDRS.

American Association of Collegiate Registrars and Admissions Officers and the College Board. 1980. *Undergraduate Admissions: The Realities of Institutional Policies, Practices, and Procedures*. New York: College Entrance Examination Board. ED 196 351. 86 pp. MF–$1.17; PC not available EDRS.

American Association for Higher Education. 1981. *High School/College Partnerships*. Current Issues in Higher Education No. 1. Washington, D.C.: AAHE. ED 213 323. 25 pp. MF–$1.17; PC not available EDRS.

American Friends Service Committee. 1979. *A Citizen's Introduction to Minimum Competency Programs for Students*. Columbia, S.C.: American Friends Service Committee. ED 155 200. 74 pp. MF–$1.17; PC–$7.24.

Angoff, William H. 1981. "Equating and Equity." In *Admissions Testing and the Public Interest,* edited by William B. Schrader. New Directions for Testing and Measurement No. 9. San Francisco: Jossey-Bass.

Astin, Alexander W. 1982a. "The American Freshman, 1966–1981: Some Implications for Educational Policy and Practice." Paper commissioned by the National Commission on Excellence in Education. Typescript. SP 021 801. 48 pp. MF–$1.17; PC–$5.87.

————. 1982b. "Excellence and Equity in American Education." Paper commissioned by the National Commission on Excellence in Education. Typescript. SP 022 211. 29 pp. MF–$1.17; PC–$5.49.

Austin, Gilbert R., and Garber, Herbert, eds. 1982. *The Rise and Fall of National Test Scores*. New York: Academic Press.

Bailey, Stephen. 1 June 1981. "Comment." Excerpts from speeches delivered at a seminar for the Institute for Educational Leadership, May 1981, at Hartford, Conn., in *Education Times*.

Biemiller, Lawrence. 19 January 1981a. "Iowa's Regents Reject Plan to Limit Required Tests." *Chronicle of Higher Education*, p. 8.

————. 6 April 1981b. "Test-Takers May Ask For and Get Answers to SATs Next Year, College Board Decides." *Chronicle of Higher Education*, p. 1.

————. 16 September 1981c. "The Enigma of ETS: Guardian of Privilege or Public Service?" *Chronicle of Higher Education*, pp. 5–6.

————. 30 September 1981d. "10-Year Program to Improve the Preparedness of High School Students Set by College Board." *Chronicle of Higher Education*, p. 1.

————. 11 November 1981e. "New ETS Head Proposes 'Code of Fair Testing' as Voluntary Alternative to Federal Regulation." *Chronicle of Higher Education*, p. 4.

————. 10 February 1982a. "Most Colleges Urged to Reconsider Use of Admissions Tests." *Chronicle of Higher Education*, p. 9.

————. 1 September 1982b. "Evaluators Praise ETS, Urge Steps to End Test Misuse." *Chronicle of Higher Education*, p. 9.

————. 29 September 1982c. "SAT Verbal, Math Scores Up for First Time in 19 Years." *Chronicle of Higher Education*, p. 1.

————. 13 October 1982d. "White Students Score Highest on SAT Exams." *Chronicle of Higher Education*, p. 1.

————. 20 October 1982e. "Board Says Minority Group Scores Helped Push Up Averages on SAT." *Chronicle of Higher Education*, p. 1.

————. 10 November 1982f. "Microcomputers Expected to Bring Radical Changes in Testing." *Chronicle of Higher Education*, p. 4.

————. 16 March 1983a. "College Board Drops Nine Achievement Tests in N.Y., Citing Costs of Disclosure Law." *Chronicle of Higher Education*, p. 8.

————. 20 April 1983b. "A New NAACP Program Preps Low-Income Students for SATs." *Chronicle of Higher Education*, p. 7.

Boardman, Sharon G., and Butler, Michael J. 1981. *Competency Assessment in Teacher Education*. Selected papers from the Conference on Competency Assessment in Teacher Education:

Making It Work. Washington, D.C.: ERIC Clearinghouse on Teacher Education/American Association of Colleges for Teacher Education. ED 206 570. 104 pp. MF–$1.17; PC–$11.12.

Botstein, Leon. 1 December 1982. "Beyond Great Books Programs and Fads in the Curriculum." *Chronicle of Higher Education,* p. 28.

Boyer, Ernest L. 1983. *High School: A Report on Secondary Education in America.* Report to the Carnegie Foundation for the Advancement of Teaching. New York: Harper & Row.

Boyer, Ernest L., and Kaplan, Martin. 1977. *Education for Survival.* New Rochelle, N.Y.: Change Magazine Press.

Brandt, Ron. May 1980. "On Admissions Testing: A Conversation with Fred Hargadon." *Educational Leadership:* 655–57.

Brickell, Henry M. May 1978. "Seven Key Notes on Minimum Competency Testing." *Phi Delta Kappan* 59: 589–92.

Campbell, Crispin Y. 23 March 1983. "College Bound and Black." *Washington Post.*

Carnegie Commission on Higher Education. 1973. *Continuity and Discontinuity: Higher Education and the Schools.* New York: McGraw-Hill.

Carnegie Council on Policy Studies in Higher Education. 1977. *Selective Admissions in Higher Education.* San Francisco: Jossey-Bass.

Casteen, John T., III. January 1982. "Reforming the School-College Curriculum." *Regional Spotlight.* ED 213 342. 9 pp. MF–$1.17; PC–$3.74.

Change Magazine Editors. 1979. *The Great Core Curriculum Debate: Education as a Mirror of Culture.* New Rochelle, N.Y.: Change Magazine Press.

Chronicle of Higher Education. 13 November 1979. "Major Recommendations of Foreign Language Panel," p. 11.

———. 14 October 1980a. "Carnegie Foundation Appoints 26 to National Panel on High School," p. 20.

———. 14 October 1980b. "Excerpts from Final Report of Humanities Commission," p. 14.

———. 19 January 1981a. "Undergraduate Admissions," p. 8.

———. 23 March 1981b. "Student Proves ETS Wrong; 240,000 Scores Raised," p. 2.

———. 10 February 1982a. "Text of Panel's Conclusions and Recommendations on Testing," pp. 9–10.

———. 5 May 1982b. "Maryland Colleges to Require College Preparatory Courses," p. 2.

———. 19 May 1982c. "More Campuses Emphasize General Education Courses," p. 8.

————. 16 February 1983a. "Fewer Score High on Scholastic Aptitude Test; Selective Colleges Concerned," p. 7.

————. 2 March 1983b. "Testing Service Wins Grant for U.S. Education Survey," p. 14.

————. 13 April 1983c. "Put Education at Top of U.S. Agenda, 51 Leaders Urge," p. 1.

————. 20 April 1983d. "Drop in Law Applications Blamed on Change in Test," p. 2.

————. 4 May 1983e. "California State System Begins Mathematics Tests," p. 3.

————. 4 May 1983f. "A Nation at Risk: The Imperative for Educational Reform," pp. 11–16.

————. 11 May 1983g. "Excerpts from the Report of the Task Force on Federal Elementary and Secondary Education Policy," pp. 5–8.

————. 18 May 1983h. "Stiffer Entrance Standards Approved by Mass. Board," p. 2.

————. 18 May 1983i. "Text of the College Board's Outline of the Basic Academic Subjects for Study in High School," pp. 14–16.

————. 3 August 1983j. "N.Y. Changes Testing Law to Keep Achievement Exams," p. 2.

Cohen, Arthur M., and Lombardi, John. November/December 1979. "Can the Community Colleges Survive Success?" *Change* 11: 24–27.

Cohen, Richard. 22 May 1983. "Pie Are Square." *Washington Post.*

College Board. 1981a. *Preparation for College in the 1980s: The Basic Academic Competencies and the Basic Academic Curriculum.* New York: College Entrance Examination Board. ED 212 195. 19 pp. MF–$1.17; PC not available EDRS.

————. 1981b. *Project EQuality.* New York: College Entrance Examination Board.

————. 1982a. "Improving Preparation for College in the 1980s." New York: College Entrance Examination Board.

————. 1982b. "Office of Academic Affairs and EQuality: Growing Hand-in-Hand." New York: College Entrance Examination Board.

————. 1982c. *National College-Bound Seniors, 1982.* New York: College Entrance Examination Board.

————. 1983. *Academic Preparation for College: What Students Need to Know and Be Able to Do.* New York: College Entrance Examination Board. HE 016 408. 48 pp. MF–$1.17; PC not available EDRS.

Comer, James P. March 1983. "Putting Tests to the Test."
Parents Magazine: 98.

Commission on the Higher Education of Minorities. 1982. *Final
Report.* Los Angeles: Higher Education Research Institute. ED
214 457. 47 pp. MF–$1.17; PC–$5.87.

Cooper, Charles R., ed. 1981. *The Nature and Measurement of
Competency in English.* Urbana, Ill.: National Council of
Teachers of English.

Crowl, John A. 19 January 1983. "NCAA Votes Stiffer Academic
Requirements for Participants in Intercollegiate Sports."
Chronicle of Higher Education, p. 1.

D.C. Citizens for Better Public Education. 1978. *A Handbook on
Standardized School Testing.* Washington, D.C.: D.C. Citizens.

DerSimonian, Rebecca, and Laird, Nan M. 1983. "Evaluating the
Effect of Coaching on SAT Scores: A Meta-Analysis." *Harvard
Educational Review* 53: 1–15.

Desruisseaux, Paul. 20 April 1983a. "A Scholar Teaches History
of Rock-and-Roll—and, in the Process, the Country's."
Chronicle of Higher Education, pp. 5–6.

————. 22 June 1983b. "Brown's 'New Curriculum': Going
Strong after 14 Years." *Chronicle of Higher Education,*
pp. 4–5.

Dixon, Rebecca R. 1981. "After the Test: There Should Be No
Mystery." In *Admissions Testing and the Public Interest,*
edited by William B. Schrader. New Directions for Testing and
Measurement No. 9. San Francisco: Jossey-Bass.

Down, A. Graham. 1979. "Implications of Minimum-Competency
Testing for Minority Students." Paper presented at the annual
meeting of the National Council on Measurement in Education,
11 April, San Francisco. ED 178 616. 12 pp. MF–$1.17; PC–
$3.74.

Ebel, Robert L. Spring 1982. "Selective Admission: Whether and
How." *The College Board Review* 123: 22–24.

Farr, Roger, and Olshavsky, Jill Edwards. April 1980. "Is
Minimum Competency Testing the Appropriate Solution to the
SAT Decline?" *Phi Delta Kappan* 61: 528–30.

Farrell, Charles S. 26 January 1983a. "A Critic Sees His Protest
against Racism in Sports Vindicated after 20 Years." *Chronicle
of Higher Education,* pp. 17–19.

————. 26 January 1983b. "Two Civil Rights Leaders Denounce
NCAA's New Academic Standards." *Chronicle of Higher
Education,* p. 1.

————. 23 March 1983c. "Black Educators Call for Repeal of
NCAA's Academic Requirement." *Chronicle of Higher
Education,* p. 1.

————. 20 April 1983d. "Black Colleges Threaten Court Action to Alter NCAA's New Academic Rules." *Chronicle of Higher Education,* p. 13.

————. 4 May 1983e. "Desegregation Goals Lead Three Virginia Universities to Extend Deadlines for Black Applicants." *Chronicle of Higher Education,* p. 18.

————. 11 May 1983f. "Federal Commitment to Excellence in Education Urged by Panel." *Chronicle of Higher Education,* p. 5.

————. 11 May 1983g. "Poor Quality of U.S. Education Imperils Economy, Panel Charges." *Chronicle of Higher Education,* p. 10.

Farrell, Charles S., and Vance, N. Scott. 16 March 1983. "Black Leaders Weigh Proposals to Revise Rules for Athletes." *Chronicle of Higher Education,* p. 1.

Feinberg, Lawrence. 6 April 1982a. "Robb Calls Much Virginia College Remedial Work Wasteful." *Washington Post.*

————. 22 September 1982b. "Nationwide Average on SAT Rises for the First Time in 19 Years." *Washington Post.*

————. 10 November 1982c. "Freshmen Standards for U-Md. Admission to be Raised in '84." *Washington Post.*

————. 22 January 1983a. "U. of Md. Tightens Admissions." *Washington Post.*

————. 22 April 1983b. "U-Va. Extends Deadline for Black Students." *Washington Post.*

————. 31 May 1983c. "Experts Debate Passing Score for Math Competency Tests."

————. 7 June 1983d. "Educators Debate Value of New Secondary Courses."

Fields, Cheryl M., and Jacobson, Robert L. 21 January 1980. "Nader Accuses ETS of 'Fraud,' Plans Drive for Testing Reform." *Chronicle of Higher Education,* pp. 5–6.

Fisher, Thomas H. May 1978. "Florida's Approach to Competency Testing." *Phi Delta Kappan* 59: 599–602.

Fitzgibbon, Thomas J. 1981. "Effects of Government Regulation on Testing Boards and Agencies." In *Admissions Testing and the Public Interest,* edited by William B. Schrader. New Directions for Testing and Measurement No. 9. San Francisco: Jossey-Bass.

Flygare, Thomas J. October 1981. "De Jure: Graduation Competency Testing Fails in Georgia." *Phi Delta Kappan* 63: 134–35.

Forrest, Aubrey. 1982. *Increasing Student Competence and Persistence: The Best Case for General Education.* A Report of the College Outcome Measures Project (COMP). Iowa City,

Iowa: American College Testing Program/National Center for the Advancement of Educational Practices.

Glass, Gene V. May 1978. "Minimum Competence and Incompetence in Florida." *Phi Delta Kappan* 59: 602–5.

Goodlad, John I. 1983. *A Place Called School*. New York: McGraw-Hill.

Hall, James W., and Kevles, Barbara L., eds. 1982. *In Opposition to Core Curriculum: Alternative Models for Undergraduate Education*. Westport, Conn.: Greenwood Press.

Haney, Walt. May 1980. "Trouble over Testing." *Educational Leadership:* 640–50.

Haney, Walt, and Madaus, George F. November 1978. "Making Sense of the Competency Testing Movement." *Harvard Educational Review* 48: 462–84.

Hargadon, Fred. 1981a. "Institutional Autonomy and Responsibility." In *Admissions Testing and the Public Interest,* edited by William B. Schrader. New Directions for Testing and Measurement No. 9. San Francisco: Jossey-Bass.

———. October 1981b. "Tests and College Admissions." *The American Psychologist* 36: 1112–19.

Harnett, Rodney T., and Feldmesser, Robert A. March 1980. "College Admissions Testing and the Myth of Selectivity: Unresolved Questions and Needed Research." *AAHE Bulletin* 32: 3–6.

Harris, Art. 26 April 1983a. "A Sampler of Questions from Florida Teacher Examination." *Washington Post*.

———. 26 April 1983b. "Tests Taking a Toll on Black Teachers." *Washington Post*.

Hart, Gary K. May 1978. "The California Pupil Proficiency Law as Viewed by Its Author." *Phi Delta Kappan* 59: 492–95.

Hibbs, Eleanore C. April 1980. "A State College Adopts a Program of Minimum Competencies in English." *Phi Delta Kappan* 61: 561.

Higher Education Daily. 7 April 1982a. "Campus News," p. 6.

———. 8 April 1982b. "Yale Agrees to Require Foreign Language Study," p. 5.

———. 19 April 1982c. "Schools Emphasize Writing but Need to Do More, Report Says," p. 4.

———. 19 May 1982d. "Ability Tests May Be Illegal for Handicapped, Research Council Says," p. 1.

———. 19 May 1982e. "Studies Sought on Teacher Quality and Student Achievement," p. 5.

Hilliard, Asa G., III. Winter 1979. "Standardization and Cultural Bias as Impediments to the Scientific Study and Valuation of

'Intelligence.' " *Journal of Research and Development in Education* 12: 47–58.

———. May 1980. "Educational Assessment: Presumed Intelligent until Proven Otherwise." *Journal of School Health* 50: 256–58.

———. 1982. "Minority Student Performance on Entrance Examinations." Address at the National Conference on Effective Retention Programs for Minority Students, 23 March, Baltimore, Md.

Hoffman, David. 27 May 1983. "Reagan Presses Plan for Teacher Merit Pay, Criticizes NEA Stand." *Washington Post*.

Hook, Janet. 4 May 1983a. "Raise Standards of Admission, Colleges Urged." *Chronicle of Higher Education*, p. 1.

———. 11 May 1983b. "Colleges Woo Brightest Students with Academic Scholarships." *Chronicle of Higher Education*, p. 1.

———. 11 May 1983c. "Report on Excellence in Education Acclaimed; Panelists Criticize Reagan's Interpretation." *Chronicle of Higher Education*, p. 1.

———. 20 July 1983d. "Smith and Mount Holyoke Colleges Drop Their New Merit Scholarship Programs." *Chronicle of Higher Education*, p. 2.

Hymowitz, Carol. 13 April 1983. "Colleges Start Giving Student Aid Based on Scholarship Instead of Need." *Wall Street Journal*.

Ingalls, Zoë. 7 July 1982. "Virginia Adopts Flexible Plan for Certifying Teachers." *Chronicle of Higher Education*, p. 3.

Isikoff, Michael. 27 May 1983. "Tougher Va. School Standards Urged." *Washington Post*.

Jacobson, Robert L. 13 November 1979. "New York's 'Truth-in-Testing' Law Called Threat to Quality of the SAT." *Chronicle of Higher Education*, p. 1.

———. 19 January 1981a. "Association Urged to Draft 'Standards' for College Admissions." *Chronicle of Higher Education*, p. 4.

———. 30 March 1981b. "Discovery of Second Error Poses Threat to Test, College Board Chairman Says." *Chronicle of Higher Education*, p. 1.

———. 14 April 1982a. "Personal Qualities Said to Play No Key Admissions Role." *Chronicle of Higher Education*, p. 1.

———. 30 June 1982b. "Educators Debate Wisdom of Raising College Entrance Standards." *Chronicle of Higher Education*, p. 11.

Jencks, Christopher, and Crouse, James. Spring 1982. "Aptitude vs. Achievement: Should We Replace the SAT?" *The Public Interest* 67: 21–35.

Keller, Helen. 1902. *The Story of My Life*. New York: Dell.

King, Wayne. 24 June 1977. "Stiffer Teacher Test Upsets Blacks in South Carolina." *New York Times*.

Kintzer, Frederick C., ed. 1982. *Improving Articulation and Transfer Relationships*. New Directions for Community Colleges No. 39. San Francisco: Jossey-Bass.

Kirst, Michael W. 1981. *Curriculum: A Key to Improving Academic Standards*. New York: College Entrance Examination Board.

Kissler, Gerald R. 1982. "The Decline of the Transfer Function: Threats or Challenges?" In *Improving Articulation and Transfer Relationships,* edited by Frederick C. Kintzer. New Directions for Community Colleges No. 39. San Francisco: Jossey-Bass.

Klein, Thomas, and Gaff, Jerry. 1982. *Reforming General Education: A Survey*. Washington, D. C.: Association of American Colleges. ED 216 655. 22 pp. MF–$1.17; PC not available EDRS.

Knoell, Dorothy M. 1982. "The Transfer Function—One of Many." In *Improving Articulation and Transfer Relationships,* edited by Frederick C. Kintzer. New Directions for Community Colleges No. 39. San Francisco: Jossey-Bass.

Knott, Bob. January/February 1975. "What Is a Competence-based Curriculum in the Liberal Arts?" *Journal of Higher Education* 46: 25–40.

Kurtz, Howard. 6 October 1982a. "Black SAT Scores 110 Points under White." *Washington Post*.

———. 14 October 1982b. "Minority Students' Gains Largely Responsible for SAT Score Rise." *Washington Post*.

Lerner, Barbara. Summer 1980. "The War on Testing: David, Goliath, and Gallup. *The Public Interest* 60: 119–47.

———. October 1981. "The Minimum Competence Testing Movement: Social, Scientific, and Legal Implications." *The American Psychologist* 36: 1057–66.

Lewis, Ronald H. 1979. "Do Minorities Embrace the Concept of Minimum Competency?" Paper presented at the annual meeting of the National Council on Measurement in Education, 11 April, San Francisco. ED 178 615. 12 pp. MF–$1.17; PC–$3.74.

Loacker, Georgine S. 1981. "Alverno College's Program in Developing and Assessing Oral Communications Skills." Paper presented at the 67th Annual Meeting of the Speech Communication Association, November, Anaheim, Calif. ED 212 001. 24 pp. MF–$1.17; PC–$3.74.

London, Howard B. 1978. "The Perils of Opportunity: The Working-Class Community College Student in Sociological

Perspective." In *Hurdles: The Admissions Dilemma in American Higher Education,* edited by Herbert S. Sacks. New York: Atheneum.

————. 1982. "Academic Standards in the American Community College." Paper commissioned by the National Commission on Excellence in Education. Typescript. SP 021 805. 44 pp. MF–$1.17; PC–$5.49.

McCabe, Robert H. May 1981. "Now Is the Time to Reform the American Community College." *Community and Junior College Journal* 51: 6–10.

————. 1982. "Improving Quality in Open-Admission Community Colleges." Presentation to the 30th SREB Legislative Work Conference, Atlanta, Ga.

McCombs, Phil. 22 November 1982. "NEH Backs the Basics." *Washington Post.*

McCurdy, Jack. 2 December 1981. "California Professors Recommend Program to Improve Skills of College-Bound Students." *Chronicle of Higher Education,* p. 6.

McDaniel, Thomas R. November 1977. "The NTE and Teacher Certification." *Phi Delta Kappan* 59: 186–88.

————. October 1981. "South Carolina's Educator Improvement Act: Portent of the Super School Board?" *Phi Delta Kappan* 63: 117–19.

McQuaid, E. Patrick. 11 August 1982. "Notes on . . . Admissions." *Chronicle of Higher Education,* p. 3.

————. 16 February 1983. "Test Score Use in Admissions Assailed in Mass." *Chronicle of Higher Education,* p. 7.

Madaus, George F. October 1981. "NIE Clarification Hearing: The Negative Team's Case." *Phi Delta Kappan* 63: 92–94.

Maeroff, Gene I. 1983. *School and College: Partnerships in Education.* Princeton, N. J.: Carnegie Foundation for the Advancement of Teaching.

Magarrell, Jack. 6 October 1982. "General Education Found Gaining Faculty Support. *Chronicle of Higher Education,* p. 8.

Manning, Winton H. 1977. "Educational Research, Test Validity, and Court Decisions." Paper presented at the first meeting of the American Educational Research Association, April, New York. ED 178 557. 32 pp. MF–$1.17; PC–$5.49.

Manski, Charles F., and Wise, David A. 1983. *College Choice in America.* Cambridge, Mass.: Harvard University Press.

Menacker, Julius. 1975. *From School to College: Articulation and Transfer.* Washington, D. C.: American Council on Education.

Middleton, Lorenzo. 13 November 1979. "Humanities Face Hard

Struggle in Two-Year Colleges." *Chronicle of Higher Education*, p. 3.

——. 2 February 1981. "Emphasis on Standards at Miami-Dade Leads to 8,000 Dismissals and Suspensions in Three Years." *Chronicle of Higher Education*, pp. 3–4.

——. 3 February 1982a. "Colleges Urged to Alter Tests, Grading for Benefit of Minority Group Students." *Chronicle of Higher Education*, p. 1.

——. 14 April 1982b. "Two-Year Colleges 'Beneficiaries of Hard Times.' " *Chronicle of Higher Education*, p. 2.

Milton, Ohmer, and Edgerly, John W. 1977. *The Testing and Grading of Students*. New Rochelle, N. Y.: Change Magazine Press.

Morgan, Dan. 16 January 1981. "Blacks Gaining in Writing Skill; U.S. Level Static." *Washington Post*.

Muscatine, Alison. 15 April 1983. "U-Md. Told to Tighten Entrance Requirements." *Washington Post*.

Nader, Ralph, and Nairn, Allen. 1980. *The Reign of ETS: The Corporation That Makes up Minds*. Washington, D. C.: Learning Research Project.

Nairn, Allen, et al. May 1980. "Class in the Guise of Merit." *Educational Leadership:* 651–53.

National Association for the Advancement of Colored People. 1976. *NAACP Report on Minority Testing*. New York: NAACP Special Contribution Fund.

——. 1983a. "NAACP Positions on Testing." Typescript. New York.

——. 1983b. "Test Preparation Clinics for Disadvantaged Black Youth." Typescript. New York.

National Commission on Excellence in Education. 1982a. "College Admissions and the Transition to Postsecondary Education." Staff analysis of the visit to Chicago by the National Commission on Excellence in Education, 23–24 June. Typescript. SP 022 069. 31 pp. MF–$1.17; PC–$5.49.

——. 1982b. "College Curriculum: Shape, Influence, and Assessment." Staff analysis of a panel discussion conducted by the National Commission on Excellence in Education at the University of Rhode Island, 27–28 August, Kingston, R.I. Typescript.

——. 1983. *A Nation at Risk: The Imperative for Educational Reform*. Washington, D. C.: Government Printing Office. SP 022 181. 65 pp. MF–$1.17; PC–$7.24.

National Education Association. 1982. *Resolutions, Legislative Program, and Other Actions 1982–83*. Washington, D. C.: NEA.

National Public Radio. 1981. "Getting into College," *Options in Education*, Program No. 307–308. Washington, D.C. ED 212 225. 26 pp. MF–$1.17; PC–$5.49.

National Research Council. 1982. *Ability Testing: Uses, Consequences, and Controversies*. 2 vol. Washington, D. C.: National Academy Press.

National Science Board. Commission on Precollege Education in Mathematics, Science, and Technology. 1982. *Today's Problems, Tomorrow's Crisis*. Washington, D. C.: National Science Foundation.

———. 1983. *Interim Report*. Washington, D. C.: National Science Foundation.

Neill, Shirley Boes. 1978. *The Competency Movement: Problems and Solutions*. American Association of School Administrators Critical Issues Series. Sacramento, Calif.: Education News Service.

Olive, Ralph. October 1978. "The College that Made Milwaukee Famous." *Change:* 10.

Parrish, William C. 1980. *State-Mandated Graduation Requirements*, Reston, Va.: National Association of Secondary School Principals.

Paul, Angus. 13 April 1983. "Student Decisions about College . . . " *Chronicle of Higher Education*, p. 23.

Perry, Suzanne. 27 October 1982. "Admissions Officers, under the Gun, Urge Faculty Members to Help Them." *Chronicle of Higher Education*, p. 25.

Peterson, Bill. 8 February 1983. "Academic Gap Found Narrowing." *Washington Post*.

Phi Delta Kappan. May 1978a. "Friends Service Offers Advice on Minimum Competency Testing" 59: 625.

———. May 1978b. "National Education Groups Form Testing Coalition" 59: 646.

———. October 1981. "ETS Announces Plans to Revise the National Teacher Examination" 63: 83.

Pipho, Chris. May 1978. "Minimum Competency Testing in 1978: A Look at State Standards." *Phi Delta Kappan* 59: 585–87.

———. 1981. *State Activity Minimum Competency Testing*. Denver, Colo.: Education Commission of the States. ED 187 715. 35 pp. MF–$1.17; PC–$5.49.

Popham, W. James. October 1981. "The Case for Minimum Competency Testing." *Phi Delta Kappan* 63: 81–91.

Popham, W. James, and Rankin, Stuart C. December 1980. "Detroit's Measurement-Driven Instruction." *Educational Leadership:* 208–9.

Powell, Brian, and Steelman, Lala Carr. February 1983. "Equity and the LSAT." *Harvard Educational Review* 53: 32–44.

President's Commission on Foreign Languages and International Studies. 1979. *Strength through Wisdom: A Critique of U.S. Capability.* Washington, D.C.: U.S. Government Printing Office.

Raspberry, William. 1 April 1983a. "Better Tests—Or Better Scores?" *Washington Post.*

————. 27 April 1983b. "So What If the Tests Are Biased?" *Washington Post.*

————. 2 May 1983c. "In Search of Better Teachers." *Washington Post.*

————. 13 May 1983d. "These Are the Basics?" *Washington Post.*

Resnick, Daniel. 1982. "History of Educational Testing." In *Ability Testing: Uses, Consequences, and Controversies,* vol. 2. Washington, D. C.: National Academy Press.

Rockefeller Commission on the Humanities. 1980. *Final Report.* New York: Rockefeller Commission.

Rutherford, F. James. 13 April 1983. "The Dangerous Decline in U.S. Science Education." *Chronicle of Higher Education,* p. 64.

Sacks, Herbert S., et al. 1978. *Hurdles: The Admissions Dilemma in American Higher Education.* New York: Atheneum.

Schinoff, Richard B., and Kelly, J. Terence. 1982. "Improving Academic Advisement and Transfer Articulation through Technology." In *Improving Articulation and Transfer Relationships,* edited by Frederick C. Kintzer. New Directions for Community Colleges No. 39. San Francisco: Jossey-Bass.

Schrader, William B., ed. 1981. *Admissions Testing and the Public Interest.* New Directions for Testing and Measurement No. 9. San Francisco: Jossey-Bass.

Scully, Malcolm G. 3 February 1975. "No Grades, No Credits, but 40 'Competence Units.' " *Chronicle of Higher Education,* p. 5.

————. 15 October 1979a. "College Board Cuts SATs in New York, Citing State's New Law on Testing." *Chronicle of Higher Education,* p. 2.

————. 13 November 1979b. "Require Foreign Language Studies, Presidential Panel Urges Colleges." *Chronicle of Higher Education,* p. 1.

————. 14 October 1980. "Improve the Quality of Schools, Humanities Commission Urges." *Chronicleof Higher Education,* p. 1.

————. 13 April 1981a. "General Education Called a Disaster Area by Carnegie Officials; Need for Revival Seen." *Chronicle of Higher Education*, p. 1.

————. 9 December 1981b. "Entrance Rules Tightened at Some Public Institutions." *Chronicle of Higher Education*, p. 1.

————. 11 May 1983. "Raising College Standards Is Already 'In the Works.' " *Chronicle of Higher Education*, p. 1.

Shane, Harold G. October 1977. "The Academic Score Decline: Are Facts the Enemy of Truth?" *Phi Delta Kappan* 59: 83–86.

————. 1981. *A Study of Curriculum Content for the Future.* New York: College Entrance Examination Board.

Shields, Mark. 13 May 1983. "Teaching vs. the Teachers' Union." *Washington Post.*

Sjogren, Cliff. 1982a. "College Admissions and the Transition to Postsecondary Education: Standards and Practices." Paper commissioned by the National Commission on Excellence in Education. Typescript. SP 022 069. 31 pp. MF–$1.17; PC–$5.49.

————. 11 August 1982b. "Wanted: More Flexible Admissions Policies." *Chronicle of Higher Education*, p. 15.

Southern Regional Education Board. 1977. *Lateral and Vertical Student Mobility: An Essential for the Community College.* Atlanta, Ga.: SREB.

————. 1979. "The Search for General Education: The Pendulum Swings Back." Issues in Higher Education No. 15. Atlanta, Ga.: SREB. ED 179 169. 9 pp. MF–$1.17; PC–$3.74.

————. 1982a. "Preparing Students for College: The Need for Quality." Issues in Higher Education No. 19. Atlanta, Ga.: SREB. ED 214 488. 9 pp. MF–$1.17; PC–$3.74.

————. June 1982b. "Writing across the Curriculum." *Regional Spotlight* 14. ED 215 368. 8 pp. MF–$1.17; PC–$3.74.

————. October 1982c. "School-College Cooperation for Teaching Gifted Students." *Regional Spotlight* 14. ED 223 168. 10 pp. MF–$1.17; PC–$3.74.

————. 1983. "Raising Requirements for High School Graduation and College Admissions." Atlanta, Ga.: SREB.

Southern Regional Education Board Task Force on Higher Education and the Schools. 1981. *The Need for Quality.* Atlanta, Ga.: SREB. ED 205 133. 33 pp. MF–$1.17; PC–$5.49.

Task Force on Federal Elementary and Secondary Education Policy. 1983. "Excerpts from the Report of the Task Force." *Chronicle of Higher Education* (11 May 1983): 5–8.

Thomson, Scott D. 1982. *College Admissions: New Requirements by the State Universities.* Reston, Va.: National Association of Secondary School Principals.

Thurston, Paul, and House, Ernest R. October 1981. "The NIE Adversary Hearing on Minimum Competency Testing." *Phi Delta Kappan* 63: 87–89.

Vance, N. Scott. 2 February 1983a. "Testing Service Head Hits NCAA's Academic Rules." *Chronicle of Higher Education,* p. 1.

———. 16 February 1983b. "Academic Rules Would Affect Blacks Far More than Whites, Study Finds." *Chronicle of Higher Education,* pp. 17–18.

———. 9 March 1983c. "Modifications of New NCAA Rules Weighed by College Presidents." *Chronicle of Higher Education,* p. 1.

Walsh, Elsa. 19 May 1983. "Third of Montgomery Ninth Graders Fail State Math Exam." *Washington Post.*

Washington Post. 12 January 1983a. "NCAA Tightens Requirements for Athletic Grants."

———. 28 February 1983b. "Florida Test on Trial."

———. 1 March 1983c. "Frequent Testing Backed."

———. 17 March 1983d. "Computer Skills Will Be a Must in City Schools."

———. 18 May 1983e. "No Diploma for 1,300 Florida Students."

———. 27 May 1983f. "Top Maryland Students to Get Fees Waived."

Watkins, Beverly T. 2 February 1981a. "Scholars Increasingly Concerned about 'Deterioration of Literacy.' " *Chronicle of Higher Education,* pp. 3–4.

———. 23 March 1981b. "A 'Critical' Shortage of Schoolteachers Likely by 1985, Education Deans Warn." *Chronicle of Higher Education,* p. 1.

———. 29 September 1982a. "At Some Community Colleges, the 'Open Door' Begins to Close." *Chronicle of Higher Education,* p. 1.

———. 3 November 1982b. "Demand Grows for Reforming High Schools." *Chronicle of Higher Education,* p. 1.

———. 16 February 1983a. "Cooperation Said to Be Increasing between High Schools, Colleges." *Chronicle of Higher Education,* p. 1.

———. 2 March 1983b. "Wider Use of Tests Blamed for Decline in Number of Black Schoolteachers." *Chronicle of Higher Education,* p. 7.

———. 4 May 1983c. "Associate Degree Programs 'Weak' Community College Officials Say." *Chronicle of Higher Education,* p. 10.

———. 4 May 1983d. "With Increased State Aid, Two-Year Colleges Fear They Are Losing Local Orientation." *Chronicle of Higher Education,* p. 10.

————. 18 May 1983e. "Mastery of Six Basic Subjects and Six Intellectual Skills Urged for College-Bound Students." *Chronicle of Higher Education*, p. 1.

————. 1 June 1983f. " 'Wave of Reform' in Education Must Start with Schoolteachers, UCLA Dean Says." *Chronicle of Higher Education*, p. 1.

Wharton, Clifton R., Jr. November/December 1979. "The New Darwinism of Basic Learning." *Change* 11: 38–41.

White, Ronald D. 22 May 1983. "Promotions at Midterm under Fire." *Washington Post*.

Whitla, Dean K. 1982. "Value Added and Other Related Matters." Paper commissioned by the National Commission on Excellence in Education. Typescript SP 022 449. 32 pp. MF–$1.17; PC–$5.49.

Wickenden, James W. 29 September 1980. "How the SATs Are Used—and Sometimes Abused." *Chronicle of Higher Education*, p. 56.

Willens, Howard P., et al. 1975. *"United States of America, Plaintiff, and North Carolina Association of Educators et al., Plaintiff-Intervenors, v. State of North Carolina et al., Defendants.* United States District Court for the Eastern District of North Carolina, Raleigh Division, Brief Amicus Curiae for Educational Testing Service." ED 121 806. 74 pp. MF-$1.17; PC–$7.24.

Willingham, Warren W., and Breland, Hunter M. 1982. *Personal Qualities and College Admissions*. New York: College Entrance Examination Board. ED 215 636. 263 pp. MF–$1.17; PC not available EDRS.

Winn, Ira Jay. 2 March 1983. "Colleges Must Stop Blaming Schools and Start Examining the Causes of the Crisis in Education." *Chronicle of Higher Education*, p. 64.

Witty, Elaine P. 1982. *Prospects for Black Teachers: Preparation, Certification, Employment*. Washington, D. C.: ERIC Clearinghouse on Teacher Education. ED 213 659. 40 pp. MF–$1.17; PC–$5.49.

Wynter, Leon. 14 January 1983a. "Board Stiffens Requirements in P. G. Schools." *Washington Post*.

————. 27 May 1983b. "Three of Four Ninth Graders Fail P. G. Math Exam." *Washington Post*.

Zibart, Eve. 25 April 1983. "Fairfax High School Gifted Program Sparks Debate on Elitism." *Washington Post*.

Zigli, Barbara. 28 April 1983. "Top Scholars Are Wooed Like Athletes." *USA Today*.

ASHE-ERIC HIGHER EDUCATION RESEARCH REPORTS

Starting in 1983 the Association for the Study of Higher Education assumed co-sponsorship of the Higher Education Research Reports with the ERIC Clearinghouse on Higher Education. For the previous 11 years ERIC and the American Association for Higher Education prepared and published the reports.

Each report is the definitive analysis of a tough higher education problem, based on a thorough research of pertinent literature and institutional experiences. Report topics, identified by a national survey, are written by noted practitioners and scholars with prepublication manuscript reviews by experts.

Ten monographs in the ASHE-ERIC/Higher Education Research Report series are published each year, available individually or by subscription. Subscription to 10 issues is $50 regular; $35 for members of AERA, AAHE, and AIR; $30 for members of ASHE. (Add $7.50 outside U.S.)

Prices for single copies, including 4th class postage and handling, are $6.50 regular and $5.00 for members of AERA, AAHE, AIR, and ASHE. If faster first-class postage is desired for U.S. and Canadian orders, for each publication ordered add $.60; for overseas, add $4.50. For VISA and MasterCard payments, give card number, expiration date, and signature. Orders under $25 must be prepaid. Bulk discounts are available on orders of 10 or more of a single title. Order from the Publications Department, Association for the Study of Higher Education, One Dupont Circle, Suite 630, Washington, D.C. 20036, (202) 296-2597. Write for a complete list of Higher Education Research Reports and other ASHE and ERIC publications.

1981 Higher Education Research Reports

1. Minority Access to Higher Education
    Jean L. Preer

2. Institutional Advancement Strategies in Hard Times
    Michael D. Richards and Gerald Sherratt

3. Functional Literacy in the College Setting
    Richard C. Richardson, Jr., Kathryn J. Martens, and Elizabeth C. Fisk

4. Indices of Quality in the Undergraduate Experience
    George D. Kuh

5. Marketing in Higher Education
    Stanley M. Grabowski

6. Computer Literacy in Higher Education
    Francis E. Masat

7. Financial Analysis for Academic Units
    Donald L. Walters

8. Assessing the Impact of Faculty Collective Bargaining
    J. Victor Baldridge, Frank R. Kemerer, and Associates

9. Strategic Planning, Management, and Decision Making
   Robert G. Cope

10. Organizational Communication in Higher Education
    Robert D. Gratz and Philip J. Salem

1982 Higher Education Research Reports

1. Rating College Teaching: Criterion Studies of Student Evaluation-of-Instruction Instruments
   Sidney E. Benton

2. Faculty Evaluation: The Use of Explicit Criteria for Promotion, Retention, and Tenure
   Neal Whitman and Elaine Weiss

3. The Enrollment Crisis: Factors, Actors, and Impacts
   J. Victor Baldridge, Frank R. Kemerer, and Kenneth C. Green

4. Improving Instruction: Issues and Alternatives for Higher Education
   Charles C. Cole, Jr.

5. Planning for Program Discontinuance: From Default to Design
   Gerlinda S. Melchiori

6. State Planning, Budgeting, and Accountability: Approaches for Higher Education
   Carol E. Floyd

7. The Process of Change in Higher Education Institutions
   Robert C. Nordvall

8. Information Systems and Technological Decisions: A Guide for Non-Technical Administrators
   Robert L. Bailey

9. Government Support for Minority Participation in Higher Education
   Kenneth C. Green

10. The Department Chair: Professional Development and Role Conflict
    David B. Booth

1983 Higher Education Research Reports

1. The Path to Excellence: Quality Assurance in Higher Education
   Laurence R. Marcus, Anita O. Leone, and Edward D. Goldberg

2. Faculty Recruitment, Retention, and Fair Employment: Obligations and Opportunities
   John S. Waggaman

3. The Crisis in Faculty Careers: Changes and Challenges
   Michael C. T. Brookes and Katherine L. German